"Capone's latest book opens with a prologue that establishes its central, unifying theme. In it, she explains that the title of the work was inspired by the story of the 'little engine that could'; it's fitting, she says, because it's how 'love seems to have shown up in my life: underdog love, tenacious love—small love that turns into big love.' Over the course of sixty-five pieces, the author examines how various aspects of love have touched her life. Her subjects include her bond with her adoptive family, her volunteer work with her church and an organization that aids girls in Guatemala, her trips to Italy with her husband, and the importance of friendship and finding connections with others. . . . Capone's Christian faith is a central element of many essays . . . and she delivers her spiritual messages with nuance and grace. . . .

"A thoughtful, inspiring collection that may appeal to fans of Erma Bombeck's and Anne Lamott's work."

—Kirkus Reviews

"Capone's humorous and faith-laced autobiographical anecdotes arguably cast a wider net than variants on the theme of love. . . . The book imparts sage messages of wisdom that come from age and having experienced the highs, the lows, the anguish, and all the happiness that life has to offer. Simple messages such as a smile goes a long way; making amends and saying you're sorry should be on one's daily to-do list, not on one's bucket list; children have a voice; one is never too old to learn something new; and there are ample rewards in random acts of kindness.

"While some of these may sound like bromides . . . they are given new life when seen through Capone's witty and energetic perspective. The engine behind her advice is her spirited prose, which has the power to change one's own point of view as well as transcend demographics.

"Whether in need of entertainment, inspiration, or merely a different perspective on life in general, *The Little Love That Could* has something that will fit each bill, for a recommended blend of memoir and self-help."

—Self Publishing Review

"This collection of over sixty mainly autobiographical short pieces . . . might be understood as gentle sermons . . . or prayers. Reading Pamela Capone's brief essays is like having a heart-to-heart conversation over a cup of tea with a kind, funny, honest friend who has emerged from a life touched by sorrow with her heart gloriously intact.

". . . *The Little Love That Could* is a refreshing reminder that faith and joy exist within an honest accounting of our imperfect days. This series of personal and faith-based essays compassionately guides readers through the doubts and struggles to a place of greater peace, appreciation, and understanding.

"IR VERDICT: In *The Little Love That Could*, author Pamela Capone is passionately committed to using her own life experience—written in accessible, compassionate prose—to help, advise, and heal."

—IndieReader

"Pamela Capone shares her epiphanies in a moving collection of personal essays that explore the power of love and her transformation from orphan to child of God. . . .

"When loving foster parents took her in, she was filthy and malnourished, a self-described ragamuffin who spent decades overcoming the belief that she was unlovable. Now a hip, gregarious California powerhouse in her mid-50s, Capone confides that it took God's unconditional love to set her straight.

"Mixing the style of a motivational speaker with evangelical zeal, Capone reveals herself as a kind, generous woman who has mastered the skill of turning small talk into big conversations. Each chapter is a modern parable ending with a lesson about tenacity, forgiveness, generosity, and God's grace. . . . Capone pulls from personal experiences, Eastern spirituality, self-help gurus, Bible verses, and pop culture, even using invented words . . . when traditional vocabulary fails. Together, these elements create a warm, entertaining, and edifying read.

"Although Capone's male, Christian God may not be everyone's deity, her insightful, good-natured stories represent the best of human nature, sharing universal truths that can be appreciated by people of all cultures."

—Blueink Review

"An amazing compilation of wonderful stories that inspire love for self and, more importantly, for others. Through her family experiences and wonderful friendships, Capone shows how love can change and empower lives. . . . She also includes friends' stories, people who have given up their comfort for the benefit of others, and meaningful historical accounts such as that of Rosa Parks. The stories are filled with beauty, love, and courage. They show what simple acts of kindness and pluck can achieve. . . . They also touch on social issues, and the accounts reveal deep-rooted problems that can be solved through compassion and putting others first. . . . *The Little Love That Could* is a must-read for anyone longing for some warmth and inspiration."

—Readers' Favorite

"Pamela Capone's *The Little Love That Could* is a spiritual autobiography told in vignettes—about living with your own flaws, choosing to be a helpful force in the lives of others, and expressing gratitude for blessings. . . .

"The book imparts its perspective well across its many different stories, reinforcing connections between Capone's faith and her daily reflections. Life lessons come through in an endearing, self-critical but good-humored tone. . . . Capone's revelatory vulnerability around her own tendency to be too sensitive and her bouts of impatience result in original takes on common subjects such as marital spats and gratitude for life's gifts. Gentle self-mockery . . . and colloquial phrases . . . lighten the tone in a pleasing way. . . . The end result is a cohesive, satisfying memoir."

—*Foreword* Clarion Reviews

WHAT INDIVIDUAL READERS ARE SAYING ABOUT *THE LITTLE LOVE THAT COULD*

"Incredibly captivating, *The Little Love That Could* is filled with inspirational stories, and thought provoking and faith-filled messages written in the most unique and transparent style. Author Pamela Capone takes us on a journey through her life, giving us a front-row seat to her best memories, painful difficulties, and *aha* moments, causing fresh hope to rise within a reader's heart. Her positive outlook on life, mixed with a sense of humor, makes each chapter easy to read and relate to in a personal way. This book will revive your heart to beat again, no matter how many of life's challenges may have knocked you down.

Allow *The Little Love That Could* to strengthen your soul to live fully awake and dream with eyes wide open, bigger than ever before . . . . It sure did it for me!"

—**Ceitci Demirkova,** founder & CEO, *Changing a Generation*; author of the best-selling, award-winning book, *Motivated by the Impossible: Recognizing Your Invisible Mentors*

"Capone did it again. Only this time—in her follow-up book to *I Punched Myself in the Eye*—Pamela Capone digs deeper, mining tougher subjects, sometimes unearthing intimate matters of her own heart. Her willingness to go there can perhaps inspire others to risk and be a little more vulnerable too. In that place is where we find the gold."

—**Jim McNeff,** police lieutenant (ret.); author; partner and managing editor, *Law Enforcement Today*

"Not many of us take the time to stop and think about our day in any real, meaningful way, but Pamela Capone's new book, *The Little Love That Could*, encourages us to do just that—to consider how small, seemingly unimportant interactions and events in our lives actually have real meaning. The book is an entertaining reminder to not only stop and smell the roses, but to stop and examine how our actions impact loved ones and strangers, and how our attitudes and way of living can and should encourage hope, promote love, and inspire others. *The Little Love That Could* is an excellent, inspiring book that should be required reading, especially in these divisive times."

—**Libby Kirsch**, Emmy award-winning reporter; author of the Stella Reynolds and Janet Black Mystery Series

"I love the way Pamela Capone sees people. Reading *The Little Love That Could* gives us a glimpse into the love that fills her soul. She delivers intriguing stories that are relatable and leaves us wanting more. Each chapter invites us to look at life through a different lens, perhaps giving us a new way to look at people and situations, to remind us to not let potentially meaningful moments pass us by. Her book is perfect for those who need a reminder that we are all capable of great acts of love—and these can sometimes come from the tiniest of moments."

—**Mary Creager** (M.Ed.), adjunct professor, Becker College

"Amazingly, after writing *I Punched Myself in the Eye*, Pamela Capone still has more humorous and profound wisdom to share with the world. That's what *The Little Love That Could* is for. In this potent work, Capone starts off by sharing some intimate stories from her barefoot childhood. Drawing upon the insights gained from the senior citizens with whom she visits regularly, philosophical giants such as Victor Frankl, passages from the Bible, and especially her own life experience, she shares her peculiar view of the world with the intent of lifting others to a higher plane. If you're looking to learn from a woman who offers advice such as 'Eat the gnocchi' and 'Memorize a joke' as well as inadvertently getting a handbook on how to become a better human being, then *The Little Love That Could* is a must-read."

—**Sean Marshall,** author of *A Council of Angels*

"Another home run for author Pamela Capone. If you liked *I Punched Myself in the Eye*, you are going to love *The Little Love That Could*. With her unique humor and charm, Capone takes us along on her journey in a most delightful way. From the streets of Italy to a storm shelter in Texas to running through the streets of Riverbank, her stories are so vivid that you will see them unfold before you. Told in a way that only Capone can, she makes each story come alive. You will love this heartwarming book, and trust me, you will not want to put it down. Well done, Pamela."

—**Lucy DeCaro,** business professor, College of the Sequoias

"I love Pamela Capone's writing. . . . I literally laughed out loud in several of the chapters. Not just smiled and silently giggled, but a hearty, *make-some-noise* laugh. Those moments are coupled with moments of introspection and inspiration. I love Capone's transformation of the term 'stranger' to 'the Unmet,' leaving the potential for a future friendship. Ideas like that are offered with insight and humor and will make us all believe that *Love Can*."

—**Vicki McCarty,** indie film producer/talent manager, Covington International

"In this book that is easy to read, personal, honest, and very touching, Pamela Capone uses a wonderful blend of heart and wit to share her valuable insights into life and love."

—**Jay Grant,** pastor of Little Church by the Sea (Laguna Beach, CA)

"*The Little Love That Could* provides snapshots of Pamela Capone's life where she finds love, forgiveness, and redemption. Her 'ragamuffin' origin allows her to connect to the hearts of those around her, including hundreds of little Guatemalan IMA girls. Capone shows that despite our differences, there are some things that transcend language, culture, and age. Her words inspire us to see the God-given treasures that are all around us."

—**Jamie Randy,** president, International Medical Assistance (IMA)

"This is a delightful read. Pamela Capone weaves the threads of her life—the funny and the painful—into a colorful fabric of insightful essays. She's an emerging, fun author."

—**Brad Johnson,** pastor of California Community Church (Agoura Hills, CA); author of *The 4 Laws of Forgiveness*

"Pamela Capone's writing is brilliant, hilarious, self-deprecating, and wise. This delightful book is filled with vulnerability and courage and deep joy."

—**Jeff Tacklind,** pastor of Little Church by the Sea (Laguna Beach, CA); author of *The Winding Path of Transformation*

PAMELA CAPONE

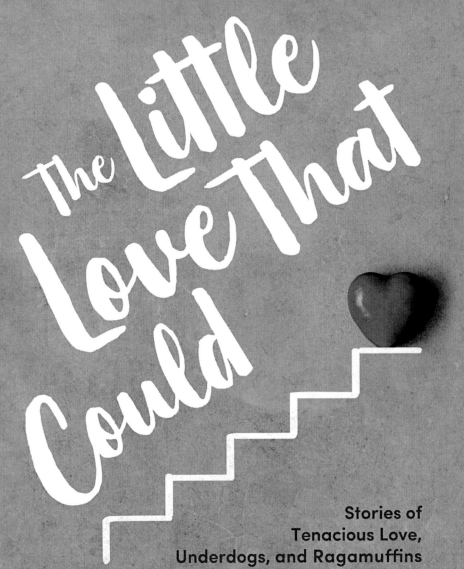

The Little Love That Could

Stories of
Tenacious Love,
Underdogs, and Ragamuffins

Aha!
Press

Contents

To Brooks,
my biggest,
newest little love

The Little Love

Sitting with my extra-small, sweeter-than-cotton-candy, ninety-three-year-young friend Inez, I mention to her that I've begun a new book. Her feet not quite touching the ground in her armchair, she lights up like a teeny firecracker—the kind where you don't anticipate a *BOOM!*

"Oh, you *have*? Delightful! I'm so glad! You know, Pam, you have a natural flow to your writing. Reading your words is like talking to you! I can just see and hear you on the page. It's like I'm right there with you!"

She goes on to remind me again of the night she read my previous book, *I Punched Myself in the Eye,* for the first time: "I had an awful cold that New Year's Eve, and surely didn't want to pass my bug onto anyone else! So I had to decline *all my invitations* and figured I'd just need to stay home to usher in the new year. I don't think I've ever been alone on a New Year's Eve, but I made my calls and apologies. Well, there I was, getting ready to watch the ball drop in Times Square all by myself, when I remembered that I'd just received your book! Once I began to read, I completely forgot that I was sick as I chuckled over and over again. The hours just flew by. Oh, I tell you, it was just the nicest New Year's, Pam, spent with you."

Her warm, enthusiastic smile never broke as she spoke. And my heart swelled at her ebullience.

"Well, I've only drafted a few chapters so far, and I hadn't come up with a potential title until yesterday," I admitted. "Lately I've been a little discouraged, honestly. *I Punched Myself in the Eye* has received so much critical acclaim, but selling it to the masses is another story. Yesterday, though, I thought, *That book is kind of like 'the little engine that could.'* And then I heard this phrase in my mind: *The Little* Love *That Could.* And it just sounded so sweet to me, and so perfect for the way love seems to have shown up in my life: underdog love, tenacious love—small love that turns into big love." I looked at my friend very intently. "Even now, sitting here with you, Inez, I see that *you* personify what I'm talking about. I look at you, so little in this big recliner, and all I can see is the big love you exude, filling you up, filling us all up. Any chair you sit in is automatically a *love*seat. Your very being represents that sort of big-little love."

This book is about teensy-weensy firecracker love that, when activated, produces a burst of fireworks. It's about feet-on-the-ground love. Sky's-the-limit love. Life-changing, world-engaging, mustard-seed love that grows from an idea, an epiphany, a hunch, a nudging from above, and then blossoms in the willingness of a heart to act on its sometimes-wobbly faith. Such audacious, underestimated love that just keeps chugging along over "impossible" hills, sweating and sputtering, shrugging off the naysayers, imagining the view from the top, is the stuff of legend. May my words put a little fuel in your tank to help you get up and over—to see that all things are indeed possible . . . if we believe *Love can.*

"I just never gave up hope."

—BOB WILEY

What about Bob?

Ragamuffin

ragamuffin *noun* A person, typically a child,
in ragged, dirty clothes.

I've heard countless times what I was like when my mom and dad brought me home as a toddler: I was filthy.

Gesturing like a Major League pitcher with her arm, my mom reminds me, "I took that dirty bottle you were sucking on and threw it out the door." I think she wanted to get it as far as the east is from the west. (She reminds me of Someone Else.)

She put me in the bath and scrubbed me, shampooing my blonde ringlets. According to the story, which I do not doubt, I left a ring around the tub.

She didn't have anything else for me to wear, so she put me in my new big brother's way-too-big footie pajamas.

She says I was ravenous, so she fed me. I ate like a piglet, and was partial to watermelon and tomatoes.

She took me to the doctor, and he said I was malnourished.

She called her sister and asked for my new, older cousin Susan's hand-me-downs.

She says her mom—my new grandma Josephine—gave her money to buy me some clothes. My mom purchased frilly dresses that were just my size.

She says I was now unrecognizable.

She says my new older brother and sister, Danny and Cheryl, ran around the neighborhood telling everyone who'd listen that their mommy had a baby. The neighbors were confused.

I think I was too. She says I cried all the time. (She will sometimes say it twice for emphasis: Cried. All. The. Time.)

She held me.

She wiped my tears.

In all the years she's been recounting those early days, I have never felt shamed by her description. I've felt loved by the details. By the lengths she went to transform my sorry state.

She took me—an undernourished, homeless, orphaned ragamuffin—into her home and into her arms. She loved me *as* her own because, in one teeny, life-changing moment, I *became* her own.

Her split-second decision to become my mom was my first example of *a little love that could*, because she had a little love that *would*. I think that might be the way it works: the willingness.

As a toddler, I was unable to remove my "filthy rags" and clothe myself in pretty dresses. I needed my momma. The prophet Isaiah of the Bible says I also need my Father. As a believer, God clothes me too—He clothes me in righteousness. Isaiah says my heavenly Father does for me what I cannot do for myself. *My* attempts at righteousness are like those filthy rags my new mom removed that day she brought me home.

God has brought me home and so transformed my sorry state that I am unrecognizable in the very best of ways. And dressed as His beloved—His little beloved—I now sport a jeweled tiara on my blessed, ragamuffin head. And I am new.

Amygdala Airlines

G ood evening. Welcome aboard."

I did a double take at the striking redhead as we boarded our Delta flight returning home from Jamaica. A little later on, she passed by my aisle seat, offering snacks and beverages.

"Excuse me, were you on a Delta in-flight safety video awhile back?" I asked.

Smiling a heard-this-question-before-smile, she replied, "That'd be me. Glad to hear I haven't aged that much."

I did an abbreviated Kip "Yesssss!" from *Napoleon Dynamite*, pulling my fist down to my side. "I knew it!"

Back home in California, I did my homework (also known as a Google search): "Delta In-Flight Safety Video Girl." *Tap, tap, tap* . . . Her actual red head, name, and face popped up.

I travel a lot for my work as a professional, though unpaid, people watcher. It comes with the territory. I fly with ordinary folk just like me, and I've flown with celebrities. One time I passed *The Bachelor*'s Jake Pavelka as I returned from the lavatory on a flight. He was wearing his American Airlines pilot's uniform, though he wasn't actually our pilot on the flight.

Prior to the Delta In-Flight Girl was *Third Rock from the Sun*'s John Lithgow on a flight back from NYC. Dude was downright amiable. At other times there was Natalie Morales from *The Today Show*, quietly reading; *Baywatch* hunk David Hasselhoff being all tanned and handsome; and once, the bigger-than-life Bobby Brown alongside us in coach.

While standing behind Bobby in line as we were boarding our LAX-to-JFK flight, it became clear to me, based on his ongoing snarky commentary, that his reputation preceded him. He even went so far as to *suggest* to my husband, John, that he was putting his carry-on in an overheard compartment not designated for him. Bobby had a point: John *was* putting his bag in a space that was technically reserved for first-class customers. For some reason, though Bobby didn't have a first-class seat himself, he felt it was *his prerogative* to make a point. Seemed to me, Bobby wasn't really staying within his Hula-Hoop either.

I get it. I have sometimes had a hard time minding my own business. I tend to want to right wrongs. Especially as a child, I'd have the weight of my *own* world on my shoulders, and then I'd add some of the world's weight, just so I'd be good and stooped.

I was told I was a little (a lot) too sensitive. I interpreted that as being a little broken. Something was wrong with me that I felt emotions so intensely. Today, I'm well aware that one of the ways I self-sabotage is to overthink. Which often leads to "overfeeling." I can easily end up dealing with some unnecessary negative emotions because I thought too much about a problem—and most times there was no real problem until I made it one—er, well, until Amygdala made it one. Amygdala is the li'l culprit inside my brain that takes situations into her own hands, hijacks things, says its fine to get outside my Hula-Hoop . . . *Go ahead.*

Sometimes Amygdala transitions from Girl Gone Wild to full-on Terrorist with a Russian Accent, just like that. What's so tricky is that I'm typically unaware when she's gone rogue. Like an airplane hijacking, at first the flight might be like any other—you're all buckled in and have your peanuts and ginger ale, but sooner or later you find out the plane has been commandeered.

In the film *Air Force One*, Harrison Ford plays United States president James Marshall, who shows the terrorist there's a new marshal in town when he chucks the scary Russian out the door. But not before growling, "Get off my plane," not unlike Clint Eastwood's "Get off my lawn." I want to growl to Amygdala, "Get out of my brain." Or more accurately, "Go back to the part of the brain you belong in: the touchy-feely district, not over here in neocortex where it's all business. I love you, I need you, but you're out of bounds, sister!"

I've seen my share of hijacking movies, but none more powerful than *United 93*. I've probably watched this depiction of the 9/11 hijack at least a half dozen times, and there hasn't been one time that I didn't sob uncontrollably at the ending. The sights, the sounds, the emotions—all capturing such bravery-amid-fear as the passengers rushed the cabin and overtook the cockpit . . .

The intensity of the final scene reduces me to a puddle. The passengers—those flying "angels"—were able to obtain their objective *while in the throes of great emotion but still using logic*. Somehow, miraculously, they blended both.

I would sure love to learn to do the same.

Table Talk

I had lunch today with my friend Inez. We sat at a round table in the corner of her assisted-living residence dining room, a community that assists the memory impaired. It's a beautiful place. It really is. The staff are friendly, respectful dignity givers.

Up until this move a few weeks ago, Inez had been on her own. A well-traveled, independent woman, she is of Puerto Rican descent and spent much of her life in the publishing industry in Manhattan before she moved out West. She's savvy, educated, proper, refined, elegant, gracious, loving, beloved. She's teeny, but she's so, so huge.

We enjoy some standard banter. I give her a compliment, and she smiles coyly and says, "Oh, I don't know about that," and I say, "Oh, I know about that!" She smiles again. And I do too. And we leave it at that.

Today she sat to my right, and on *her* right was "Robert" in his electric wheelchair; and then the second "Robert," a navy vet and retired attorney; and then "Marilyn" and Marilyn's beau, "West"; and then back to me. My sweet friend ordered a chicken salad sandwich with potato chips and coffee with cream, one sugar. I had the bland cup of low-sodium chicken orzo soup and a plain iceberg salad with a few shreds of carrot, ranch dressing on the side.

In a way, it was a people-watcher's paradise—an airport and Disneyland all in one place. It was tough to take notes, however. I didn't want to be rude. Plus, words pretty much escaped me. So I sat, absorbed, engaged.

My heart broke; my heart filled. I watched struggles with manipulating forks, too-full water glasses, scattered thoughts, revisited words just spoken.

Much of the conversation was on a continual loop. The first topic was the election. Marilyn and West were Hillary supporters. That was clear. Marilyn was the ringleader, the outspoken one—raising her hand to punctuate her position, sometimes rolling her eyes or shaking her head. She recognized that First Robert, across the table, would cancel out her vote with his Trump. I wasn't clear who Second Robert was endorsing. He talked mostly about missing his wife. My sweet friend Inez, well, she was demure and wasn't sure if her new move meant she was no longer registered to vote. She was troubled by this election. None of it sat right with her.

The most interesting of the group, I have to admit, was Marilyn. She looked like Hollywood. Blonde curls, unbelievably smooth skin, thick Angelina lips, and once-bright blue eyes, perhaps some enhancements *up top*. But still, so incredibly natural and beautiful. I couldn't take my eyes off of her. I asked her what she did for a living, and she said she had been a schoolteacher in Los Angeles.

Early on in the meal, I had asked West if he and Marilyn were married. I had noticed them stealing some looks, along with toasting empty wine glasses (several times). The only wine glasses on the lunch table. A wide grin spread across his face. "No, she's my girlfriend."

"Ah," I said.

Her eyes agreed.

When I'd first sat down, I had introduced myself and asked Marilyn her name. She replied, "Mac." First Robert looked at me and said in a matter-of-fact tone, "She's not Mac. Her name's Marilyn." Marilyn/Mac rolled her eyes and shrugged her shoulders.

After politics was exhausted as a topic, I got a little of everyone's backstory, including Second Robert's. He and his wife were married fifty years, and she's now been gone eleven. Every time he said that line, he was a notch sadder. But he does have a new lady friend. They go to church together, but they're just friends—nothing romantic. They'd never *live together.*

Marilyn shrugged, interjecting, "Too bad."

There was a whole lot of quiet. It was too quiet for me. In fact, I felt uncomfortable. Until I didn't.

I scanned the dining hall. These folks seemed fine with it; maybe I should too, I surmised. The quiet was not just devoid of words but actually peaceful. So I eased into it.

Holding her empty wine glass, Marilyn seemed to be summoning the server. I told her I'd get the server's attention. Also, First Robert needed some tending to. The fried egg sandwich he'd ordered over-hard was over-over-easy, and now it was all over him. He just waited, though, yellow goo covering his shirt and napkin. He was unruffled, like he was okay either way, yoke or no yoke.

Wine glasses now refilled, West and Marilyn were toasting his red to her white again. In fact, over the next half hour or so, they retoasted/reclinked at least a dozen times, with the same flirtatious grins and nods. At one point, I noticed a piece of food on West's lower lip, and a few moments later, Marilyn touched her napkin to his face, wiping it away.

Until my own memory fades, I will savor today's lessons of unabashed flirting, of easing into unapologetic quiet, accepting a gentle pace, of patience over inevitable broken yokes, and of voices given to respectful opposing political viewpoints, as we sat around a round table and broke bread together, not a bland flavor in the circle.

Charades and Blindspots

At Thanksgiving 2016, our family made a pact that no one would talk about the recent Trump-versus-Clinton election. This was a very good idea.

And there was another very good idea. Rather than playing a board game or charades, my nephew Jared wrote some questions on little pieces of paper and put them in a bowl. Someone would extract a scrap and read the question, and then we went around the room, taking turns answering. This turned into one of the best post-turkey activities ever. I think we all learned some pretty valuable things about each other.

One of the questions we answered was, "If you learned you had one year to live, how would you spend that year?"

I said I would be very busy, and listed some of my action items:

- Say sorry to anyone I need to.
- Deal with any unfinished business.
- Finish any project left undone.
- Tell people I love them.

Riding my bike a few days later, I thought about the foolishness of waiting until I know I'm going to die before making amends. I didn't have to jog my memory to know the two or three people I needed to call. And so I parked my bike and sat down on a very "conveniently placed" bench. Coincidence? *Nah.* It's like God pulled out a seat for me and said, "Go ahead."

And so I did. I made the first call, and it felt good. Cleansing. Then I got back on my bike and rode a little longer, feeling a lot lighter, thinking I was done for the day with this brave apology business. Until I realized I wasn't. So I hopped off again.

The Thanksgiving Q&A was the impetus, certainly. But what really got me off my bike was a glaring moment of clarity about one of my blindspots.

What exactly was evident in the window of that moment? Which blindspot became easier to see? I think—*no, I'm sure*—my ego is more often involved than I've dared to admit when I have relationship troubles. A big slice of my hurts are self-inflicted, borne out of self-protection and self-interest, when I'm attempting to present a false image—a charade.

I recently had a bike rack installed on the back of my MINI Cooper. This colossal rack is so disproportionate to my tiny coupe that it looks as if the weight of it could tip the nose of my car toward the sky. It took a while for me to get used to the rack because it created a second blindspot for me, and I was already a little paranoid about the one the car has, on the back right. After a few weeks of carting around this add-on, I'd moved from anxiety to a more comfortable awareness—an awareness I can work with, live with. Still, with this additional blindspot, I take much greater care when navigating the Los Angeles freeway system.

Now that I have acknowledged my emotional blindspot and made myself accountable regarding my tendency to self-protect, perhaps I will be that much more careful navigating the people I love too.

A *charade* is defined as "an absurd pretense intended to create a pleasant or respectable appearance." I don't want to play that game anymore. Rather, I'll keep asking myself the important questions and try to be more aware of any cumbersome things I may be carrying.

Spoiler

Just recently there was a collective, national reeling over a primetime TV show, NBC's *This Is Us*. Spoilers abounded.

A terminally ill William and his biological son, Randall, took a road trip from New Jersey to Memphis. This father wanted to show his grown son (whom he had recently become reacquainted with after leaving him at a fire station as an infant) the places of his past. William wanted Randall to know him better. He wanted to return home, make amends, introduce his son to extended family, pay respects.

There is a sweetness to this episode that pierces me. To me, Randall was already a wildly likable character, but for some reason, his "God bless you's" to strangers in Memphis almost felt like an ethereal message.

The show depicts our common humanity, communicating in so many rich ways that *It's just us. Here we are.* So yeah, good going on that title, NBC. We're hurting—and hurting each other—big time on Planet Earth right now, and we need this message more than ever.

It's been quite the hero's journey, this saga of biological father and son. Early in the season, we watched Randall search for and find William. At first, Randall had anger and mistrust and questions. Questions like why? and how could you? *How could you leave me?*

I get it.

William offers no excuses, just reasons. Honest, regret-laden reasons. I think that's the better of the two options.

The previous episode had highlighted Randall's lifelong struggle with panic attacks. On this road trip with his biological father, the son vulnerably explains his anxiety. He tells William how his deceased adoptive dad, Jack, used to help Randall cope as a child: Jack would hold Randall's face in his hands and help him breathe. "Breathe with me," he would say. Looking directly into one another's eyes, they would breathe together until the boy's panic had passed.

William asks Randall to tell him more about the father who raised him. Randall responds that his dad was larger than life; tells William about Jack's fabulous, free laugh. William asks where Jack is buried, and Randall says he was cremated. A portion of his ashes are with his sister; the rest were sprinkled at his dad's favorite park near a tree. William convinces Randall to take a half-day detour to visit Jack's resting place, teaching his tightly wound son a little about *Carpe diem*—you roll down the window, crank up the music.

From both directions, the dialogue in the car is tender, fluid. What grabbed my attention was the thoughtful, reverent way William asked about the man who stepped in, who raised his son. William seems to have no trouble referring to Jack as Randall's father. He is not threatened by him but, rather, appreciates him.

This scene reflects the way my parents, Joe and Jean Ciarolla, spoke of *my* biological parents. They never said one thing about my birth mother and father that wasn't bathed in compassion. In my case, they had plenty of reasons to diss them had they wanted to. But they didn't. Not once.

William and Randall reach the park, and William asks Randall for a private moment to pay his respects. Throughout the season, we've heard many of William's deep regrets, but here, he is in an "it is what it is" moment. Sitting on a bench, he talks to his son's father. With a clear head and open heart, he speaks:

"Thank you . . . for doing what I couldn't. . . . For raising him to be the man he is. . . . I'm sorry I didn't get a chance to meet you, *brother*.

I would have liked to hear that laugh . . . would have liked to have met my son's father."

(Me: *Gulp.*)

Satisfied that he's said just enough, William winks, nods, and concludes with, "Yeah. Cool." Standing up from the bench, he walks back to Randall, saying, "I like him."

When I was a child, it was common knowledge that I'd hit the lottery by having Joe and Jean Ciarolla take me in as their own: essentially, I'd gone from squalor to a palace. So sometimes people would comment that I was now "spoiled." I knew they said it not because I exhibited bratty behavior (I didn't. Take my word), but because they were clumsily trying to say I was "lucky" or "blessed." I knew I was these things. But "spoiled" didn't sit right with me. It singled me out, like I was undeserving, less-than.

Now I can embrace my "spoiled" status because I understand that "spoiled" means deeply loved. My *mom and dad* spoiled me rotten. They've loved me long and well. I know this has been, by extension, a spoiling by my eternal Father in heaven, and I welcome that for sure.

I've noticed how we deal with those we love who are suffering. In our awkward attempts, we overthink, obsessed with having *just the right thing to say or do* to fix it. Which doesn't. What I learned in Lamaze class years ago still stands: "Show up, and help your beloved breathe."

Near the end of the episode, William is on his deathbed in a hospital. What Randall's dad did for him as a boy, Randall offers to William. When Randall sees the dying man's fear, he draws near, holds his face in his hands, and says, "Breathe with me." It's a full-circle, precious moment, helping his dad pass on to another world. A world where there are no regrets. A world where he will most certainly be spoiled.

Bare My Sole

I don't love you anymore."

The words stung as sharp as when I'd stepped on a bee that one summer day with my tender, bare feet years before. Faces forward, he and I sat side by side on a small, wooden bench against the back wall of my parents' house on Reed Road—only now it was a little dark and a lot cold.

He spoke without turning his head.

I was nineteen; he was in his late twenties. He was my first real boyfriend—and with a beard no less! It took me too long to fall in love with him, and I guess he was tired of waiting. But I *had* fallen. I'd been afraid to say "I love you" because I knew it meant something.

That was my first big romantic heartbreak. The first, but not the last. Turns out, life includes that. If we risk.

He wanted to still hang out as friends. I told him that was going to be tough.

I cried for him long and hard. Eventually I moved on.

I won't say his name, but it rhymes with *Heaven*.

As a kid, I used to go barefoot spring through fall. By the end of the day, the bottoms of my feet would be as black as our recently paved country road. When we first moved to Oakdale from Los Angeles, the road was dirt. My mom might deny it if you ask her, but I'd often go into town with her with naked feet, walking around the five-and-dime with my black soles. At one point, I remember her insisting that I put shoes on. I ruined a lot of washcloths at bath time.

But when I was home? Baby, those feet were free! I was Kevin Bacon–footloose. Dry concrete, wet concrete, blacktop, garden soil, regular old dirt, gravel, grass, mud from the irrigation water in the vineyard out back . . . I could spread my toes and watch the syrupy clay squeeze up through them, covering my sweet, soppy digits. I'd run up and down the vineyard rows in dramatic fashion so that the splashes were bigger.

I stepped on a bee there once too. It didn't stop me. I'd sit between the vine rows, cross-legged, belly-button-deep in sludge, making mud pies. Later, when my dad had professional sprinklers installed, it was both exciting and disappointing. I wouldn't have the lengthy pools to run through, but I did have the sound of the *chhhhhhh chhhhhh chhhhhh* while I got sprayed from overhead. Even now, when I hear the *chhhhhhh chhhhhh chhhhhh* anywhere, I think of our vineyard and the sounds of summer.

At first our (what I considered) massive horseshoe driveway was simply dirt. I have a clear memory of the day my dad brought home a gargantuan Rhodesian Ridgeback dog named Simba. I believe I was five, six at the most. As I stood dead-center in the dusty driveway, Simba's ridgeback was eye-level to me, and from quite the distance, he charged me as if I was in his crosshairs, knocking me flat on my back and trampling me. I kid you not, I remember lying flat on my back, dirty bare feet up, and watching his underbelly fly over me.

No matter; I forgave him. I loved that dog. His ridge felt like an imperfection—a beautiful one. Barefoot, I rode him like a horse. He knew I could take it.

Later, as he did with the sprinkler system, Dad upgraded our dirt driveway to gravel. We were movin' on up. I remember the sound the tiny rocks made when someone would drive onto our property. In summer, the gravel became a fire walk: I'd run over the pebbles in a blur, my feet barely touching. I learned to ride a two-wheeler, and my back tire would spit tiny rocks like a semi-truck on the highway.

In the center of our horseshoe driveway was a patch of grass dotted with cherry trees and apricot trees, and up above, a treehouse built by my big brother. I climbed that tree up the wooden slats with my bare feet, which gave me better grip.

Even though the bottoms of my feet were filthy and often marred by gravel burns and splinters and bee stings, they got tougher. The feel of the earth, the traction, the grip—was worth the trade-off.

I was driving down our paved Orange County road the other day listening to Amy Winehouse's haunting rendition of "Will You Still Love Me Tomorrow?" That song's been on my priority playlist for years and reminds me of how I lived my life for a long time.

Back then, I wasn't sure I'd be loved tomorrow. While I was given lots of proof to the contrary, proof that Love could (and would) last, I worried that it might go away any day. Because the *other* proof had happened first—before "Heaven," back in LA, before the dirt roads—when I was abandoned by my biological parents.

This newer Love (courtesy of my foster parents) worked hard, proving over and over and over again that it would remain. Eventually I believed. I made progress. I began to trust. I knew I'd get burnt here and there. I'd be stung by bees and poked with rocks, and I might occasionally get trampled, but I might also be refreshed on a hot summer day by a sprinkling from overhead.

Even as an adult, I still think it's the better choice to go barefoot. I like the feel of being free—my exposed, tender, not-so-tender skin touching the ground in spite of the dangers when I bare my soles . . . and my soul.

The Bio-illogicals

I joke that, after having ten other kids, they took one look at me, looked back at each other, and said, "No, we're good. We need to stop here. STAT."

Robert and Elsie Cole weren't what you'd call *strategic* about having children. They couldn't feed us, for one thing. So there's that.

Out of the gate, Elsie's parents weren't thrilled at her ragamuffin love interest: an orphan who seemed, I'm guessing, a little sketchy. She disappointed her parents so much so that they disowned her, and she too took on orphan status.

The young couple married at city hall. Starting out their wedded life in New York City's Greenwich Village, they were contemporaries of Jack Kerouac and the Beat generation. They were both artists, and talented ones at that. Free spirits. Bohemian hitchhikers who conceived their first child on the way to California.

Throughout my childhood—a childhood I spent separated from the two of them except for brief visits—Robert Cole sent me his fictional stories and drew cartoons on the outside of the envelopes. I was secretly impressed with his talent. Although I didn't want to be.

I hated the way they'd sign their letters: "Love, Mommy and Daddy"; "Love, your ol' dad." Like we were so tight.

I eventually tossed out all of their correspondence because it reminded me of loss. I now wish I'd kept those letters and stories. Some of the things you do when you're young, you just can't undo.

I felt a lot of shame attached to my bio-illogicals. I have about a hundred thousand photos on my Facebook of family and friends, and I never considered posting a picture of my bio-illogicals. Not until now.

I saw a photo of them for the first time not so long ago, and it's the first one I've liked. It captured something (strength) and avoided something that every other picture did capture (weakness). Also, I can now admit: I see my likeness in his face. *This is huge.*

Elsie Cole always had this signature, chin-pointed-upward smile that would send me through the roof growing up. For the longest time, when I'd see someone with a similar sort of grin, I'd wince. Her smile looked to me like she was trying to convince the camera that she was proud. I wanted to say, "You're not fooling me."

At the same time, I believed she *was* proud, which seemed really illogical. They lived in a fantasy world and were, for all intents and purposes, writing their fiction. They repeated in letters how they'd get all us kids back so we could live together as a family.

They tried. I have a visceral memory of having to go to court when I was fourteen. I was horrified. HORRIFIED! I remember sitting across from them in the cold hallway at the Los Angeles County Courthouse. I could literally see Elsie's heart pumping in her chest. I wanted to look away, but I couldn't *not* look. It was like viewing a car accident.

The judge asked if I wanted to go back to live with my bio-illogicals, and I said emphatically, "I DO NOT, and if you send me there, I will run away." As timid as I was, I didn't have to muster a "Bring it!" attitude. It was an organic, don't-mess-with-me, I'll-walk-this-talk absolute. I meant it as much as I'd meant anything in my fourteen years.

Elsie died two years later. Robert died five years after that. They both passed early due to heart-related ailments. They died of broken hearts is my best guess.

I had monster nightmares about them growing up, though during our visits I remained a very polite little girl who never told them what I really wanted to say. Their choices, however, wreaked havoc. Up until my late twenties, I hated them for what they'd done.

Even after I'd stopped blaming them, it took me a long time to sever myself from the umbilical cord of shame. I thought I would be forever tethered to them. I imagined myself floating around in space like George Clooney in *Gravity* . . . *but* attached to the shuttle of Robert and Elsie. My bruised body would keep smacking against their hard surface, more and more battered with each collision.

There have been many levels and layers to my healing. At one point, I had a dream that replaced the nightmares. Rather than the familiar monster, Elsie appeared in heavenly perfection. Her eyes were no longer tired—they were bright and alive. Her skin was like porcelain, her hair flowing like an angel's. Most of all, her smile had no upward tilt of denial. It only held love.

I believe they loved us in their ragamuffin, broken-hearted way. How they showed their love was not logical, but it was their version. And while it was insufficient for this little ragamuffin girl, I'm convinced they weren't bad people.

This is how I've come to see Robert and Elsie Cole. This is how God has helped me make sense of what was once incomprehensible to me.

I no longer carry shame because I am free of the tether. God saw *my* heart, beating in my chest, and with His healing touch, He brought calm to the chaos and clarity to those years of confusion. He is the only one with an Undo keystroke, and He freely used it in my story. Still uses it to this day.

I saw evidence of another layer of healing today, in my ability to post a photo of them on Facebook. I would never have imagined this. But I did it. And I forgive them. Dare I say, I love them. As illogical as that may sound.

Water's Falling from the Sky
(Thoughts as Another Holiday Season Begins)

Water's falling from the sky; the tree is up, and there's a roaring fire in the fireplace . . .

Yesterday, just after my husband got the tree upright, I heard him put on Christmas music and start hanging ornaments. All on his own. In previous years *(all of them!)*, there's been a tug-of-war about our tree-decorating schedule. Hubby's preference would be to do it in stages: One day, get the tree. Next day, get the lights going. Next day, maybe throw on some ornaments . . . You see what I'm getting at.

Momma no likey. Momma likes to slam-dunk the tree. In one flurry of action. So this year, as I was finishing up folding some laundry and waiting for him to get the tree situated so we could jam and slam, I heard Bing Crosby. I looked out at the living room through the bedroom doorway, and there my husband was—decorating, concentrating—with a sweet look on his face.

I joined him, and we began hanging ornaments together. The porcelain ones commemorating our son's and daughter's births, as well as the ones the kids made when they were teeny, fashioned with construction paper and drippy Elmer's glue, featuring their little preschool faces. Plus there were all the other delicate trinkets and treasures collected over the years. I thought of shattered ornaments along the way, because that's how life is. One year, the entire tree fell over.

And yet, here we are. And water's falling from the sky; the tree is up, and there's a roaring fire in the fireplace. Which means I'm feeling sentimental; deeply grateful for all the things that are still shining and upright after so many years—all the delicate, fragile valuables that remain unbroken. But I am aware that's not the case for everyone, as I too have known firsthand. For some, the holidays are a threadbare, lonely stocking hanging from the mantel, maybe a little singed from the fire.

While I am so very grateful, I also want to remember those who are feeling alone—or are alone—during the next month. Including those who have had great loss this year and will face the holidays without that sweet person. And those in physical or mental pain. And those who can't afford to buy their kids a gift this year. And those dreading the days between now and when the glittery ball descends in Times Square. And those without someone to smooch that night, or under the mistletoe in these next few weeks. And those who, because of the holidays, will have rain falling from their eyes.

Let me be sensitive in my celebration. Let me include those who might be dreading this season, and be kind to those who don't expect to enjoy it but who are struggling to simply *endure* it. In my words, in my prayers, at my table, and around my tree, may I invite them to be warmed by my fire, precious and new members of my family.

Five Minutes and Fifteen Seconds

Every time I pull out of the Mother's Market parking lot carrying fresh juice, I do so with great caution because I remember that one time I hit the dip a little hard and dumped both of my thirty-two-ounce juices. I now take my ginger juice gingerly.

This week, just a few days before Christmas, I was pulling out onto Paseo de Valencia at dusk when I noticed someone RIGHT on my tail, flashing his headlights. In my rearview mirror, I could see the man flailing his arms at me and clearly yelling within the confines of his car. I was dumbfounded at his reaction until I realized he had probably been behind me when I exited the parking lot and taken that dip a little too slow for his liking.

I considered my options, one of which was offering him a single digit. Another was slowing down to a crawl. I did neither. (Okay, I'm human; maybe I slowed a bit.) Instead, as the lane next to us opened and he was able to pass, I quietly said, "Merry Christmas . . . " along with a term of endearment that may have canceled out the *Merry Christmas*.

A few thoughts also came to mind:

1. My having to take the curb slowly maybe delayed his exit by fifteen seconds. Or less.
2. He had no idea I had two full, thirty-two-ounce, highly stainable juices in my car that could easily take a tumble.

3. Trying to understand his logic, I wondered, *Did he really think his behavior would get him somewhere? Like, did he really think I would go against human nature and respond by speeding up?*

There is a video that's recently gone viral of a woman berating a woman who is in line ahead of her at JCPenney. I imagine these women were Christmas shopping. *'Tis the season. Peace and goodwill and all of that.* The berater was upset because a friend had joined the other woman in line, adding some items to her purchase, which amounted to probably an additional wait of five minutes. This so enraged the woman that she WENT OFF, making racist remarks and gesturing wildly.

It was horrible to watch.

The problem with such immediate overreaction is not just the angry person's rush to judgment but their unawareness of what might be happening in the life of their "target." My road rager this week had no idea that I was carrying juice. The JCPenney ranter had no insight into the other woman's life either.

What's apparent to the eyes is only part of the story. Someone might be "carrying" something you don't see. So, as the saying goes, "Be kind, for everyone you meet is fighting a battle you know nothing about."

Merry Christmas. Period.

On Loan

I have the worry gene.

As a child, I worried about things that I suspect most kids did not. Things like if I'd have to go back to live with my biological parents or get to stay with my foster family. Things like not missing a single day of first grade so I wouldn't get in trouble somehow, because if I did get in trouble, I might have to leave the family I loved. (This fear was born in my own broken heart, not brought on by anything my foster family did or said.)

As an adult, if I had to pinpoint where that gene spends most of its time, I'd have to say it's on my children. They are its favorite place to hang out, all sprawled out with a super-sized tub of hot, buttered popcorn in front of a big screen of my kids.

In theory, I know worrying helps nothing and only hurts. I've told this gene ad nauseam, "Hey, you're unproductive. Get out!" But it just looks over its little genie shoulder, stops chewing for a moment, raises its little genie hand, and says, "Talk to the chromosome."

I try my best to guilt the worry gene. Beat it into submission. Call it names such as "Faithless," "Joyless." But it doesn't give a rip. It's not motivated by shame or "should." However, I've found something that does help. I tend to forget about the availability of this little, freeing truth: *My kids are not really mine to begin with. They are on loan.*

I'm not sure why, exactly, but this helps me loosen my grip. Or helps loosen the worry-grip on my worst-case-scenario-prone heart. I remember this truth and, for a moment, its power puts that bad genie back in the bottle.

I think the poet Kahlil Gibran would concur. He said, "Our kids don't belong to us, really; they pass through us. We are merely the vehicle." So I guess you could say, parents are the ultimate Uber.

If you believe James of the Bible (and I do, but sometimes I forget), our lives are a mist—we're here for a brief time, and then *kapoof*, we've moved on to eternity. And it's not just us and our kids that are only around for a time, but all this stuff. All our valuables.

My house, my cute little red MINI Cooper, even my health, I don't own. It's all on loan. And the global stuff that's happening beyond my control? Well, I can do my part: raise my voice, vote my conscience, not add to the chaos, lend a hand, spread love.

In the end, it will not have mattered that I had perfect attendance in first grade, or that I worried about my kids. Because none of it's mine. It's all His.

Confliction

Like the rest of us, I awoke to the headlines that Debbie Reynolds had passed on *the day after* her beloved daughter, Carrie. Both talented performers. Exit stage left. Dramatic, painful poetry. This is what a mother's love can look like. One day without her daughter was one day too many.

I used a word last night with my daughter, Cassie, and we immediately gave each other that raised-eyebrow look as if to question, *Is that a real word?* The word was "confliction." And yes, it's real. As real as it gets. Because a mother said so.

It is also the exact word to describe the *good + bad + ugly + beautiful* equation that comprises motherhood.

A scene in a recent *Vikings* television series episode demonstrates probably the most poignant visual/cinematic representation of a mother's love that I've ever seen. While the mother's love itself is sure, pure, and unwavering, the experience of *mothering* is a little trickier.

Having known this agonizing love from the inside out, I was oddly comforted, validated, and simultaneously horrified to see what it might look like for someone else. My hope is that this scene might provide a window for someone who does not understand. Someone who might judge motherly love as irrational. Someone who has not walked in Debbie's mom-slippers.

In the *Vikings* episode, against his mother Aslaug's tearful protestations, Ivar chooses to accompany his father—the once great, now shamed King

Ragnar—on a voyage of vengeance, a raiding party to England. While Ivar wails in fright, battling the stormy sea and potential doom (something Aslaug foretold), his mother experiences it too, through something like a real-time vision or dream. What he endures, she endures. She's touched his skin, and in the scene, she bleeds for him, both literally and figuratively.

I can say the same. I was born with eczema, a dry-skin condition. As I've gotten older, it's a little better, but at times it still feels unbearable. What's worse is that I've passed it on to my kids. I see it flare up on their precious skin and I feel it on my own, because it's shared skin.

I am convinced, whether the relationship is by umbilical cord or a ballpoint pen put to adoption papers, this is what a mother's love can look like . . . feel like . . . actually is.

A few days ago, December 26, was my friend Stacie's birthday. On her Facebook wall I posted a photo of the two of us sitting on her couch, and I included the caption "Celebrating and missing your sweet, precious life, and massive impact on mine." Stacie's mom replied to my comment: "Ahhh, Pamelina, you are reminding me of how it is possible to be happy and sad at the same time."

Sweet, sour confliction.

A mother's love can be profound pleasure and great agony—the best and the worst—all at the same time. Like Aslaug's torment over her drowning son *and* Debbie's next-day-departure to meet up with her sweet girl, Carrie, it's a simultaneously horrible, beautiful, rational, irrational, incomparable love bound up in skin that we have shared, loved, and touched.

Achilles' Heal

We know of an Achilles' heel as a weakness. That one, nagging area that doesn't seem to let up or go away. The one we hate. The one we think separates us, deems us inferior.

As the Greek myth goes, Achilles' mom, Thetis, was given the worst news: her baby would have a short life. I know the lengths I will go to save, protect, and help my kids thrive, so I get Thetis. I think Thetis would get *me*.

Mom took baby boy to the River Styx in hopes that its magical waters would make her son invulnerable. Holding him by his heel, she dipped him in the river, and the water washed over him. All but the heel.

Achilles grew to be a man who fought and survived many battles, but in one he was hit with a poisonous arrow. It stuck in his heel—the only unprotected area on his body—and killed him.

Great story as stories go, but in real life? It's a tragedy.

I like the apostle Paul's take on weakness. I like this guy because he is just so *real*. He points to a happier ending. A different kind of outcome. A "healing" in a way—not the initial healing he'd hoped for.

Would it be obnoxious to quote from my own book?

> Even the apostle Paul had trouble with this one. In my interpretation, it's one of the more squirrely, relatable Scriptures in the Bible. To the Romans, he's like (and I'm paraphrasing), "Hey, I'm

just gonna put it out there—there's no good in me as far as my nature goes. I want to do what's right—I really do—but I can't. I don't want to do what's wrong, but I end up doing it anyway. Sheesh! So if I do what I don't want to do, I am not really the one doing wrong; it's that crummy, no-good nature in me that's to blame. Blame THAT.[1]

That was me, quoting me, quoting Paul.

If I read the actual passage about self-control in Romans chapter 7, I feel less crappy about myself after I do something *again* that I didn't want to do. Unfortunately, I'm actually better at admitting screw-ups in theory and talking about them later. *Much* later—when no one else remembers what I did. And then the person's like, "Oh, *that*? That was nothing. I'd forgotten all about it." *Ding ding!* Winner, winner, chicken dinner!

Truth is, in the moment, when I'm called out, I'm defensive. I think I may have found a reason why.

I just started reading Kristen Neff's book *Self Compassion*.[2] I landed on something quite revolutionary when I read the part about having compassion for myself not only when I'm hurting, but when I'm *hurting* as a verb—as in, hurting others.

Huh? Come again?

Yep:

When I'm a jerk.

When I'm entirely at fault.

When I mess up.

When I hurt someone else.

Isn't that backwards?

Neff writes about our struggle to actually recognize pain in ourselves and have compassion for that pain: "When our pain comes from

---

1 Quoted in Pamela Capone, *I Punched Myself in the Eye: Stories of Self-Sabotage, Imperfection, and Perfect, Amazing Grace* (Amazon CreateSpace, 2015), 109-110.
2 Kristin Neff, *Self Compassion: The Proven Power of Being Kind to Yourself* (New York: William Morrow, 2011).

self-judgment—if you're angry at yourself for mistreating someone, or for making some stupid remark at a party—it's even harder to see these moments of suffering."[3]

In my way of viewing, if I feel guilty, I deserve it, right? So when I do the wrong thing, I self-flagellate and self-sabotage because, you know, it's more productive to punish myself than to embrace my oops-I-did-it-again imperfection. I didn't even know I deserved compassion for making a mistake, saying a mean thing, doing that bullheaded, ornery thing Paul wrote to the Romans about way back when. I thought I deserved a metaphorical smackdown by my own hand, not a tender touch.

I love Paul's vulnerability, his honesty. Today I think we'd call him self-reflective, self-aware, maybe an evolved, new-millennium man.

To another group, the Corinthians, he spoke of his weakness—a "thorn in his flesh." His Achilles' heel. Initially he asked God to remove it. God told him that he would not remove this thorn because it provided a place for His grace. A space for His tender touch that covered Paul (and can cover us) entirely.

Ironically, seeing ourselves as we are and embracing our weaknesses—those thorns and nagging Achilles' heels—actually brings us closer to perfection, giving God the opportunity to "heal" some of the humanity that ails us, showing us the lengths He will go to save, protect, and help His kids thrive.

---

3 Ibid., 11.

Let Me Call You Sweetheart

I popped into Inez's assisted-living residence, figuring I would just sit with her in her suite and chat as we normally do. Instead, as I walked into the foyer now bedecked with a towering, colorful evergreen, I heard live music booming from the dining hall and could see the residents gathered with their chairs angled toward the red-vested pianist, who was joyfully belting out Christmas tunes. Thinking that it must be an early Christmas party, I scanned the room for Inez. The first faces I recognized were "Marilyn," stationed right next to the bar, and "West," her boyfriend.

After Inez and I situated our chairs, the server asked if we'd like something to drink—"Maybe a glass of wine or some liquor"—as she handed my friend a diamond-shaped, flaky pastry. Inez accepted the treat, declining the spirit. She said she would, however, like a cola.

The pianist had switched things up from Christmas carols to ragtime and show tunes. Most of the residents sang along, though some stared blankly. Nevertheless, the room was filled with spirit, and it filled my soul.

Inez was drawn in as well. With a big smile and bright eyes, she pointed to a woman with festive feet and said, "This one's quite the toe-tapper! Just look at those toes!" There certainly was a whole lot of tappin' goin' on. "I can just see the flappers listening to this music!" she remarked.

Looking in her eyes, I could *see* that she could see. She was remembering actual flappers, beheld by her own true eyes. What was drawing me back, however, was Marilyn and West across the room. They were mesmerizing.

Marilyn was at the bar again, waiting for her red wine and West's white. I could see her mouthing "Thank you" to the server and sitting back down next to her beau, grinning. Repetitively they clinked glasses and winked and then flirted with raised eyebrows, having forgotten that they had just clinked and winked and raised brows a minute before.

The pianist began to play "Let Me Call You Sweetheart" as Marilyn and West sang along and acted out the lines:

Let me call you sweetheart
I'm in love with you
Let me hear you whisper
That you love me too

Keep the love light glowing
In your eyes so true
Let me call you sweetheart
I'm in love with you . . .[4]

At the "Let me hear you whisper" part, they seemed compelled to move in even tighter, as though they had a secret and were getting away with something. Which they probably are.

Seeing two people with their love-light glowing—even at this stage of life—moved me to tears. I lost track of how many times Marilyn visited the bar to get their goblets replenished, and I noted a shift in West's gaze. He seemed to grow a little concerned, especially as her dance moves went slightly over-the-top. Love often looks a lot like concern.

The server came back around, and I motioned to her. She leaned in.

---

4 "Let Me Call You Sweetheart." Lyrics by Beth Slater Whitson, music by Leo Friedman, 1910. Public domain.

"Is this a special occasion?" I asked. "How often is the piano player here?"

"He's here every afternoon, but right now is happy hour, and we do it this time every Thursday."

Inez had been telling me about the pianist who comes very often, and she had said, "How wonderful it is to hear the show tunes! It just brings me back to Broadway."

How wonderful it was *for me* to be brought back to something so timeless but often neglected. To bear witness to the love-light glowing. To see eyes so true in Marilyn . . . in West . . . and particularly in my friend Inez. I'm deeply grateful for all the happy hours I've spent with her. And I'm so glad she lets me call her sweetheart.

Grasp

I didn't realize how much I loved my husband until yesterday, when I managed to schlepp a ginormous, unwieldy, forty-thousand-pound box from Costco, somehow wrap it in Christmas paper, find an actual—pretty brilliant—hiding place, and then heft it into said hiding place.

So I really must love him. A lot. Also: I rock.

Last week I asked John what he wanted for Christmas.

"Nothing," he said. "I have everything I need."

"Well, how's *that* gonna make me look!?" I whined.

"Why does it matter?"

"Because *I want stuff!*"

Since he was serious (and so was I), I figured I'd better Lone Ranger the gift shopping, because Tonto's clearly going to need something to unwrap. So yesterday I was strolling Costco, looking for ideas, when I spotted the perfect gift: a new desk chair. John has needed one since forever for his desk in the den. The low-grade leather's been disintegrating for a couple years now. *Perfect!*

Admittedly, it's a real ego boost when I'm able to flex the ol' brawny biceps and lift something large-scale myself, but when I attempted to just turn the sucker, I could see this was going to be difficult, if not impossible, to move from its tight spot on the bottom shelf and up into my cart. So when an able-bodied shopper happened to walk right past me, clearly missing his opportunity to help, I gifted him the opportunity: "Excuse me, if you don't have a bad back or anything, would you mind helping me get this box into my cart?"

With more chagrin than grin, without a word or eye contact, he obliged and muscled the cumbersome box out of the tight spot and wedged it into the top of my cart, a little askew but nonetheless secure enough.

"Thank you so much! I appreciate it!" I said, a touch over-the-top enthusiastic.

Having to now pull my cart from the side due to no visibility, I navigated the massive payload through the Costco throng, finished the rest of my shopping (which wasn't much since there was virtually no space in my buggy), checked out, and made my way to the exit where my receipt and goods were checked. (Sidebar and note for further examination: Why is it that the receipt checkers are always one of two extremes—they either meticulously line-item everything in your cart while you toe-tap and look at your watch, or they barely give your stuff a glance before swiping your receipt with the yellow highlighter? As though, at the job interview, these individuals are asked, "Do you have OCD, or are you apathetic? We need to fill both positions.")

Being the opportunity-giver that I am (see aforementioned able-bodied shopper whom I stopped in the desk-chair aisle), I ask the receipt checker, "Do you think someone might be able to help me get this box into my car?"

"Oh sure. See that red line out there on the pavement? Just leave your cart over there—it'll be fine. Pull your car up, and I'll see if I can find someone."

Considering that I had to park two counties away, and looking back to see if she'd be watching my cart—which she wasn't—I decided against her risky plan and nabbed a seemingly available, nice, strapping, red-vested young man nearby. Pushing my cart, he asked, "So, are you having a nice day?"

"I'd be having a better day if you came home with me and unloaded this enormous box out of my car."

He smiled and played along as we bantered the length of the Orange County, Los Angeles County, and Ventura County parking lot.

The chair box filled the entire breadth and length and height and depth of my MINI Cooper, bringing Ephesians 3:18 to mind. True story. As I drove home, I contemplated how I might get the box out of the car, and thought perhaps I'd ask one of my neighbor boys. But first, I'd give it a shot on my own.

I backed into the garage, aiming the rear end of the car toward my laundry folding table. Along with some other colorful narration, I sweated, grunted, and pep-talked myself, finally managing to get the behemoth cargo on top of the table, ready for the festive wrap. All the while, I was strategizing about a hiding place. This was likely the worst wrapping job I'd ever done, as pieced-together as it was, but at least it was covered, I consoled myself.

Measuring the box, I wracked my brain for options. They were few, and all had high "visibility risk." Then I remembered the storage shed in the side yard, filled with pool rafts and yard-maintenance supplies and the like. I eyeballed it. *Score! It will fit!*

I was beginning to think this could actually work, since chances were slim that John would open the shed anytime soon. It was the first time in nearly thirty-three years I was glad for his disdain for yardwork. (Sorry to out you here, John.) *Now, how to get it off the table and out of the garage and down the side yard and into the shed?* This would prove to be the most precarious and impressive feat, were I successful.

I considered the obvious: the wheel. I looked for the skateboard, and then remembered the foldable swap-meet cart—maybe I could keep it in the collapsed position, resting the box on top, kind of like a flatbed truck.

It was go time.

Positioning the flattened cart next to the table, I attempted to slide the box onto it. Gravity was not my friend. Bruises ensued.

I crawled out from underneath the box, narrated a bit more, and then pushed it onto the cart. Doing my impression of the Hunchback of Notre Dame, I slowly pulled the cart out of the garage, made my way across the sidewalk to the shed, and then tipped the box up into position and pushed it into the perfect void. *Voilà!*

A little worse for the wear, I did a victory dance. When we love someone, we sometimes pull out the stops.

Thinking back on that entire scenario now, Ephesians 3:18 comes to mind again: *Oh, if we could only grasp how wide and long and high and deep is the love of Christ.* He has gone to great lengths to show this love.

After I joined the mom club, I started running regularly to increase my stamina so that I could literally run to save my children in case there was ever some apocalyptic event. For a good while I ran ten miles every morning. I went to great lengths.

As a rule, I think real love is an exhaustive love, a fierce, protective, never-say-die love. A pull-out-all-the-stops love. A bet-the-farm love. A go-for-broke love. I've been the recipient of that kind of devotion from my parents. And truly, aside from the yardwork hitch, I've been the recipient of that kind of care and commitment from John.

These are human examples. And they all pale in comparison to the crazy love referenced by the apostle Paul in his impassioned letter to the Ephesians: *Oh, that you would know, that you would grasp* the kind of Love that can fill every void, every space, every hiding place.

I have everything I need.

Shiftless

Athletically, I'm not exactly a dork. Mathematically? Dork. But I *have* been driving a stick shift since I was a teen. I know what a clutch is.

My first bike was a red tricycle, and I'm pretty sure it was a hand-me-down from my slightly older, much cooler cousin Sue. My first brand-new bike—a two-wheeler with a fixed gear—was a pink Huffy with streamers on the handlebars. That groovy ride had a banana seat and a sissy bar and a sick wicker basket with plastic flowers on the front. So yeah, it was pimped.

I eventually got a five-speed, but no one ever showed me how to use it, and it didn't occur to me to ask how it worked, or even to investigate for myself. Riding a bike without shifting went fine, I felt. My legs worked; what else did I need?

Suffice to say, I've been riding multispeed bikes my whole life. Never, ever took advantage of shifting gears. Never used the tools. Never understood the point. Plus, with the doodads and all those numbers that came with the gears of said bikes, it definitely felt like math.

I was told that switching gears would help me go up hills, but it made no sense to me. *How would doing more revolutions be easier than just powering through on the strength of my own legs?* My husband pretty much gave up the campaign. So I've spent my life muscling up hills. On too-steep hills, for the most part, I traverse zigzag style. No big deal.

I recently got a new bike. A pricey one—a first. John gave it another whirl: "You really should use the gears, Pammy." I glared at him as he continued, "They'll help going up hills, and you're gonna ruin your chain if you don't."

That second part got my attention as I thought of the bottom number on the bike-shop receipt. I didn't completely believe John, though, so I gave him the *talk to the hand.* Still, I didn't want to damage my costly new bike, so I halfheartedly consulted an authority, my daughter. She concurred. (She always *was* her father's daughter.)

Over the phone, Cassie tried to walk me through the proper way to shift. Patiently she asked questions about my bike and about my struggle. I tried to describe the new bike to her, not knowing any of the terms for the parts. I took pictures of what I now know to be a drivetrain, cassettes, and so on, and texted them to her. I sensed she sensed I was not getting it.

She sent me a link to an REI description on how to shift gears, which I read—later. Which I still didn't get.

Equipped with that new, misunderstood, unprocessed information, I went out for a ride and came back ten minutes later, completely defeated. *How can I be this old and not know how to shift a friggin' bike?!*

I woke up the next morning, rested and with a new resolve. This was personal now. Still in bed, I busted out the YouTube tutorials. I watched video after video. Finally, one guy made sense, and the light bulb over-heard flickered. There was a glimmer of hope.

It was math all along, I said to myself. *No wonder I resisted!*

Helmet on, Asics on, fire in my belly, I began practicing with my gears on the flat-ish areas around my house, and then mustered up the courage to take on the hills (okay, *bumps*). Incorporating the information in that last YouTube video, things were starting to click. I decided to give my regular route a go, beginning with the first big hill on my street.

For the first time in my life, I didn't zigzag on that bad boy. Not once. I reached the top and could hear angels singing. It felt like a miracle and magic, all at the same time. (Sidenote: I had been frequenting a particular route since getting my new bike a few weeks prior, and had decided I would advance to a different route once I could do the whole thing without having to dismount and walk my bike up even one hill. Then and only then would I move on. And I'd made progress. But there was this one steep incline that wasn't having it, and the bike path was too narrow to traverse in my "innovated" fashion, so up until this point, I'd still had to walk it. But on this new day, I pedaled straight up each and every hill in a straight line—with not one zig or zag, and without getting off the bike path even once. I'm officially ready to move on. *Hallelujah!*)

Zipping down the hill approaching home, I realized I'd been stubbornly overworking my legs, my bikes, my heart; going out of the way; limiting myself; thinking I knew better; afraid to try something I didn't understand or see the point in; not listening to wise counsel; being unable to go as far as I'd like—all because *I didn't know what I didn't know* since forever.

It was a clutch moment. I am now Shifty Capone with a new mindset in more ways than one, ready to take on the miles and the hills on my horizon.

Black Friday

We see the headlines every year, the herky-jerky video on the twenty-four-hour news: The absurd, before-dawn throng busting through the Walmart doors, demonic eyes narrowed, headed for the electronics. Strangers literally knocking one another to the floor, some with their hands wrapped around a high-def TV . . . or around someone's neck. *Stranglers* in the night—fighting over a 75 percent-off Wii or laptop. The trampling. The swearing. The selfishness. I've even heard of bargainers getting shot.

People have died.

For real.

For presents.

For Christmas.

Two days before Thanksgiving, with the eating season just ahead, I decided I needed some new sweatpants *for expansion purposes*, so I headed to Dick's Sporting Goods. A lovely older salesperson ("Guadalupe"[5]) remarked on my nice selection while unlocking the dressing room for me. She then added that I should wait until Thanksgiving and/or the day after for the Black Friday sale. My items would be slashed by 50 percent.

I shook my head and said, "I won't be able to come on Thanksgiving, and if I wait until Friday, these might be gone," motioning to the four pairs of sweats draped over my arm. What I wanted to say was, *"Are you*

---

5 Names and places have been changed to protect the kind.

crazy? I hate shopping on a good day! I wouldn't be caught dead trampled at a Black Friday sale!"

Saying nothing, Guadalupe carefully lifted the edge of the current 25 percent off sale sign on top of the clothes rack, revealing the 50 percent off, Black Friday sale sign. Visual reinforcement. Now I understood: Guadalupe was a flat-out tease.

She lifted her eyebrows as if to say, *You see what I see?*

"Okay, what if I buy them today," I complied, "and then return them on Friday to get the sale price?"

Her eyes shifted. "I don't know. I don't think they will let you. But let me go check." She made a beeline to the front desk.

I could see Guadalupe's funeral-like face as she walked back to me. From several yards away, she began shaking her head and mouthed, "No, they won't let you."

"I think I'm just going to buy them today, Guadalupe."

Guadalupe was not finished. "What if we hide them?" She made a space behind some random sportswear. "We put them here and you come back early Friday and get them. I'll be here. I'll be here on Thanksgiving Day too, and will keep watching them."

Guadalupe was working all the angles for me, to the point of offering to babysit my hidden sweats. Surely some rules were being broken here. But her commitment to and care for a stranger like me for no other reason than to help? Almost made me cry.

I admitted to Guadalupe that I had been having a really bad day, and that her kindness changed everything. She looked at me like *De nada. Don't sweat it.*

Making up my mind about the clothes, I announced, "See you at 6 a.m., Guad!" If I were a proficient winker, I would have winked. I settled instead for a knowing smile of friendship, acknowledging our upcoming Black Friday rendezvous.

Happy Hour

My mother-in-law has a wall hanging that says: *Do one thing that makes you happy every day.* In my opinion, whoever wrote that is an underachiever. So I commented to her, "I think you should do *way* more than one thing every day." Only one is low-balling it.

Let me clarify. That happiness thing is not about hedonism; it's not about self-gratification. It's about presence. And not taking time for granted.

At its core, it's not even about the pursuit of happiness, exactly. Because, as Victor Frankl wrote in *Man's Search for Meaning,* happiness should not be pursued—it must ensue. Translation: It's the natural result of a meaningful life, not the means to a meaningful life. Said another way: The more you chase happiness as an ideal, the more elusive it is, like a cat chasing its tail, a hamster on its wheel, a cat chasing a hamster on a wheel. The harder you work to fill the void, the emptier you feel and are.

In the Declaration of Independence, Thomas Jefferson wrote of our inalienable rights of life, liberty, and the pursuit of happiness. These rights are given to all human beings by our Creator. Still, I agree with Frankl that, as a rule, happiness is a byproduct when we dedicate ourselves to a cause greater than ourselves. And this kind of happiness is spelled in three little letters: *j-o-y.* Such a tiny word, but it sure packs a punch.

My pastor spoke about joy this past Sunday. I was there, in my favored spot that I lovingly refer to as "The Pew with a View." At our Southern California church, there's a side door that, when it's open, overlooks the blue ocean if you sit in the right pew. Sometimes I'll be listening to the wise words from the pulpit while staring at the sea—and then someone will reach over and close the door because they're cold. *Buzz-kill much?* It's not exactly a Christian thing to do, if you ask me. John and I will look at each other and roll our eyes, like, *Hey, here's an idea: don't sit by the door if you're cold!*

The assisted-living place that my friend Inez recently moved in to is beautiful. I told her it's like she's on a cruise ship 24-7.

I've been visiting her at "happy hour" on Thursdays because I love watching the residents *get down with their bad selves.* Last week it was the chef who broke into spontaneous dance while the ragtime pianist played on. From across the room, I saw the chef enter the dining hall, give three loud claps, and then—in front of everyone—just *bust a move.* He was so free, he was a living, breathing, dancing embodiment of Thomas Jefferson's words. He had life; he had liberty; and in the space of that moment, he seemed to be pursuing what looked a whole lot like joy. It was a byproduct of his dedication to something outside himself. In those few moments, he was giving the gift of himself to those residents.

I watched their faces beam at his verve. One woman in particular was so visibly thrilled with his display, she sparkled, her boisterous laugh so much more than mere happiness. It made me cry. It made me cry joy-tears.

Rather than pursuing happiness, maybe we ought to intentionally pursue *moments.* Stop putting things off. Start living as though tomorrow is not guaranteed. You know, seize the day.

Thinking of my mother-in-law's wall quote, I've made a few suggestions:

Use the fine china.
Take that art class.
Write the letter.
Eat al fresco.
Audition for that play.
Eat the gnocchi.

Play hooky with your grandkids at Disneyland.

Skinny dip.

Mix the salad with your bare hands.

Try good, fresh sushi even if it scares you. (Especially if it scares you.)

If you can't travel, shop at ethnic markets in your neighborhood.

Try weird food.

Ride a bike.

Send a handwritten thank-you card.

If a favorite ceramic vase is broken, glue it; don't throw it away. The crack is good.

Offer to babysit for a young couple that can't afford to pay you.

Spend money on things like wind chimes and small water fountains.

Keep the windows open, particularly if jasmine is outside.

Call and say you're sorry.

Put up a hammock.

Use it.

Memorize a joke.

Tell it.

Don't let fear rule you. Say, "You're not the boss of me."

Have friends who are too old to be your friends.

Have friends who are too young to be your friends.

When you're with your family and friends, take the Bluetooth out of your head.

Hold hands with your friends while you walk.

Go to Mimi's for breakfast, order the *Quatre Fromages Quiche*, and pronounce it exactly the way it looks.

Say it with a straight face.

Keep the door open.

If you're cold, move or put a sweater on.

Listen and look at the sea.

Come alive.

If we do, *joy* may just walk in the door and bust a move.

Crush

I was hit on by a heartthrob. This was a nice little ego boost.

It was the mid-1980s, and I was at the Warner Brothers lot in Burbank with my show-biz friend, Vicki. As a teeny girl, Vicki danced with Elvis in the black-and-white film *Harum Scarum*. Vicki had/has cred and connections at Warner Brothers, so we meandered around the lot, snuck into soundstages, and watched the filming of shows like *The Love Boat*. Then we happened upon an Oldsmobile commercial shoot.[6] Featured in the ad were Dick Van Patten and his handsome sons, namely Vincent, who was a pretty big deal—a full-fledged teen heartthrob.

We watched for a while and walked around a little more until we ended up lunching in the commissary. I noticed familiar movie and television faces, and then I spotted the Van Pattens' table across the room.

Midway through lunch, Vicki excused herself to go to the restroom. And when she did, Vincent approached. He flashed his pearlies and said, "Hi . . . are you an actress?" (He really did.)

We chatted a bit, and then he told me he was having a party that night and invited me. I said thank you, but I won't be able to make it . . . something about leaving town that day, which was true. The real reason, though, was that I had a boyfriend—the boyfriend who later became my

---

6 Check out the commercial at https://www.youtube.com/watch?v=iTflRtbtMUg.

husband, the father of my children, and my lifetime "go-to." Ultimately, still my biggest crush.

Hindsight being good and plenty, I made the right choice.

I'd first noticed Vincent in 1975, when he was on the show *Three for the Road*, co-starring Alex Rocco and Leif Garrett. I thought he was dang cute, but it was Leif who stole the show and my newly teenaged heart. I couldn't take my eyes off his cuteness, or as I would have said, his *foxiness*.

This would be one of many unrequited love affairs. I had posters of Leif on my wall, carefully torn-out *Tiger Beat* pages of his 8 x 10 face. But there were others. I'd had my first taste of puppy love with Donny Osmond a couple years before, and in fact, his song "Puppy Love" was my first vinyl record purchase, a 45 rpm. I was a decade old that day when my mom took me to the record store. This *was* truly puppy love.

Not until I discovered Elton John the next year did my love mature, when I saved my allowance and bought his *Goodbye, Yellow Brick Road* album and then later, *Captain Fantastic*. (Oh, how I thought he was!) I had it bad for Elton, with his flamboyant costumes, glasses, and that voice.

I have a vivid memory of twelve-year-old me, lying in a hospital bed being treated for pneumonia, staring at the cover of a magazine solely dedicated to him, the object of my affection. It was a gift from someone, and whoever it was, they knew I was crushing hard on Elton and that this would lift my sickly spirits.

Even so, there was someone else on my mind besides Elton. These were tricky years for me as a victim of ongoing sexual abuse. As I lay in that hospital bed with slightly bruised and bandaged forearms due to my temperamental, hard-to-hit veins, I knew the abuse had come to an end, in part because I was finally able to give a voice to a long-silenced, shy little girl. I'd only squeaked out a few words in a small voice, but it was enough to halt the abuse.

Along with Donny, Leif, and Elton, there was John Travolta—aka Vinnie Barbarino—David and Sean Cassidy, Bobby Sherman, and rock groups like The Bay City Rollers. For a variety of reasons, none of these relationships went anywhere. First reason being, these beaus didn't know I existed.

Today, John and I were on a Skype call with my cousin Jimmy, who's been living *la dolce vita* ("the sweet life") the past few years. Awhile back, he moved from his native Ohio to Italy. We share a passion for Italy. John and I were talking about plans for our next trip to the Old Country when I interrupted the topic and blurted out how Italy must really be agreeing with Jimmy because he is still just so danged handsome. And then I went further and mentioned how I had SUCH a crush on him growing up. And then I went a little further and said that maybe I still do. I did all of this in front of John, which makes it entirely appropriate. We laughed, and Jimmy blushed a little, which made him even more adorable. I also had a crush on his twin brother, Danny, which I *didn't* mention.

I crushed on quite a few guys at Oakdale High School. During my freshman year there was "Jeff," a popular senior—a football player—who, while sporting his letterman's jacket, passed by me in the hall every day at the exact same time and always smiled a smile that told me he knew I existed. One day, three or so years after he'd graduated, I ran into him in town and he asked me out. I thought my heart would explode.

The summer following my freshman year, I was at a church camp in Wichita, Kansas, and was walking alone, crossing a field. I spotted someone coming in my direction, also alone. As this person got closer, I could see he was in fact what I would call a stone-cold *fox*. As in *babe*. As in *Holy crap, you're cute*. As he got closer, and our eyes locked, his pace quickened. Surely this meant something good.

He did not stop; he did not smile; he did not say anything at all. His apparent state of underwhelm starkly contrasted with my instantaneous, besotted rapture. Still, I was a goner.

Other boys came and went in my dating life, but there was no one I did not compare to my chance encounter on that Kansas field with this new Captain Fantastic. I got to know his family through the years, and I flirted. Hard. He even flirted back, but he never took it to the next level, and since I still had that shy, quiet voice, that was that. And my unrequited crush remained.

Six years after Kansas, something changed: he saw me. He saw that I truly existed, and that I had been right in front of him all along.

Still am. And my voice has grown in strength.

For me, there have been tricky years; there have been delays and heartbreaks; there have been crushes. I have been crushed. And I've gotten back up, brushing off all the broken pieces.

To Donny Osmond's plea in "Puppy Love"—"Someone, help me, help me, help me please . . . Is the answer up above?"—I say, yeah, it is. Yeah it is, Donny. The apostle Paul wrote of an Above Love to the believers in the ancient city of Ephesus. He longed for them (and now us) to grasp how wide and long and deep and high is this love that surpasses human understanding and yet can be grasped if one's heart is open to receiving it (see Ephesians 3:16–19).

To have a heartthrob invite you to a party is a heady thing. To have human love returned is a treasure. But to be invited to an incomparable party by a forever love? A celebration in heaven like the apostle Paul spoke of to the Ephesians? Well, that's an invitation I can't refuse.

Can I Help You?

I made a new friend today. Her name is Elizabeth. We met while we were waiting for our mammograms, which I affectionately call a *pam*mogram. Also known as "The Vise."

Unrelated event: Yesterday our family doctor called. I answered the phone and he said, "Mrs. Capone? This isn't a business call. I just wanted to tell you that I saw the *USS Indianapolis: Men of Courage* movie and was so impressed with your son Joey's performance. That was a great movie, and it's a story that needed to be told." We talked for about fifteen minutes about such things. I thanked him for taking time out of his day to encourage someone else, then hung up the landline, picked up my cell, and autodialed Joey.

I relayed the doctor's words. I could tell this touched my son—that the affirmation was a shot in the arm, if you will. An authentic, unsolicited bit of *help* to his heart. It meant something that a busy physician would do it for no other reason than kindness.

Back to today: As I walked into the waiting area at the women's health clinic, my new friend-to-be, Elizabeth, was standing at the counter getting instructions from the receptionist on how to fill out her medical information on an iPad. Elizabeth had fear on her face as she walked back to her chair. I checked in with the receptionist, who said I ought to take a seat; she'd be with me as quickly as she could. She seemed busy. A little distracted, a little frazzled.

I took a chair two down from Elizabeth, who was working on her iPad. After emitting some sounds of frustration, Elizabeth walked back up to the receptionist, who curtly answered her question and then quickly went back to her busyness. Elizabeth wasn't satisfied. I looked at her as she passed in front of me, distraught. She sat down, put her iPad in her lap, and hung her head. More sounds and words of confusion, revealing her German accent. I leaned over and asked, "Can I help you?"

A look of relief spread across her face.

I showed her how to use the touch screen, but she still seemed overwhelmed, so I offered, "Maybe we can do this together." She quickly handed the tablet to me. When I realized that the questions were getting more and more personal, I asked if she wanted to tap in the answers herself. Without missing a beat, she emphatically shook her head. "No, YOU do it, please. I don't care. We're just people."

After I tapped the final field, I had learned an awful lot about Elizabeth, but I was about to learn a whole lot more. Privileged information.

Elizabeth had endured a rough patch. She'd lost her forty-four-year-old son to cancer the previous year, and she'd really been having a hard time lately. She told me how kind he was. How he helped others. "What a good man," she said.

Elizabeth leaned over to me and gave me one of the tightest hugs I've had to date. For a moment I couldn't breathe. She let go of me and told me that I am the best thing that's happened to her in a very long time. I told her the same. She said that she tries to be a kind person; helps people where she can. She tries to be the kind of person she can see that I am.

I told her I think that's one of the big reasons we're here on earth: just to help. I told her I thought that when we are paying attention, we see people who can use a hand. She wholeheartedly agreed, and then Elizabeth got choked up. I did too. In that moment, our hearts touched in a way I can't quite describe. Then the receptionist called Elizabeth's name, and we parted ways.

Another older lady across the room walked up to me and asked if I'd help her on her iPad questionnaire. I did. This lady was a doppelgänger for my aunt Bette, who passed away last year. Spitting image.

After helping Aunt Bette's twin, my name was called. I filled out my questionnaire all by myself. When I gave it to the receptionist, I told her I would be right back—I was going to run out to my car and grab something.

I passed an elderly couple moving like sweet turtles up the sidewalk, headed for the door I had just passed through. I grabbed a copy of my book *I Punched Myself in the Eye* from my trunk. Walking quickly back toward the medical building, I passed the turtle couple and then paused and held the door for them. The woman looked up at me from her walker, and she was a doppelgänger for my mom. Could have been her twin. She and her husband smiled sweetly, as though they were surprised I would wait that long to hold a door for them.

I handed my book to the receptionist and asked her if she'd give it to Elizabeth when she checks out, unsure if I'd see her again. She smiled and said she sure would. She didn't seem so busy anymore. Less frazzled. My take was that maybe she had witnessed all the friendships being made.

After being led back into the second waiting area and having changed into my pink smock with the front tie that does absolutely nothing, I sat in my chair waiting for my turn in The Vise. From the hallway, Elizabeth peeked her head around the corner, stepping in so I could see she was holding my book to her heart. She sat down next to me, and we talked a little longer. Meanwhile, Aunt Bette's doppelgänger now sat across from us in this waiting area, watching, listening, nodding.

I told Elizabeth I wanted to give her my book because, for the most part, it is about paying attention; about showing up for others, helping where we can, loving strangers, 'cause, well, I think that's one of the big reasons we're here.

Elizabeth put her arms out to me for another hug. I feared a little for my oxygen levels and my menopausal bones. As our hearts touched again, she not only got choked up this time; she full-on cried. She told me she loved me. She said, "I mean that, I really do. I love you." I repeated her words back to her. I meant it, I really did.

Right before Elizabeth walked out the door, eyes full of tears, she put her hand on her heart and said, "You have touched me in a very special way today."

After I had my turn in the vise grip that they call a mammogram, I got dressed and walked down the hall, passing the front desk. The receptionist told me how much Elizabeth loved me, how my kindness had impacted my new friend, and how in turn it had affected the receptionist herself. The receptionist—whose eyes were also filled with tears—gave me a bear hug, hearts touching.

Liberty Mutual Insurance has recently run a "Pay it forward" TV ad campaign. It's a good one, illustrating how, when we witness an act of kindness, we are inspired to help someone else in some way. Whether it's a tangible act or words of affirmation, it rubs off.

I'm relaying what happened to me today at my pammogram, not to highlight my goodness but to highlight *goodness*, to highlight *light*. Maybe Dr. Such-and-Such's call is not so unrelated to my experience with Elizabeth after all. Maybe his kindness rubbed off on me.

In our world, we're often inundated with bad news, lies, nastiness, darkness. Sometimes it feels like we're in an ever-tightening vise grip. I turn the news on, and after five minutes I need a soul shower. Dr. Martin Luther King Jr. said, "Darkness cannot drive out darkness; only light can do that. Hate cannot drive out hate; only love can do that."

So I say, let's help each other. Touch hearts. Watch. Listen. *Pay attention.* If we look closely, we can see our aunts and our mothers in others.

As Elizabeth said, *We're just people.* Joining our lights, we can make brilliance with four little words: *Can I help you?*

Hallmark

It's Valentine's Day here in Jamaica. My husband, John, and I awoke to the sound of pounding waves and reggae. He had just gotten up to go the bathroom, so I hopped out of bed and grabbed the ruby-red, wrapped gift I'd hidden in my luggage. I placed it on the covers, tucked the Hallmark card under the ribbon, and waited for his return, feeling rather proud of my stealth maneuver and eager to see his surprise.

He walked back into the room and *was* surprised. With a crestfallen face, he whispered, "Oh . . . Pammy." It was the *Uh-oh, I screwed up* face. I knew right away that he didn't get me a gift.

Ouchy.

He took a cleansing breath. "Um, I got you a card, but I haven't had a chance to sign it. I'm sorry."

A card. No mention of a present.

He stood staring at the gift and then slowly opened his card. He read the words inside, managing a weak smile, and began to open his gift.

He tried on the shirt I'd bought him; said he really liked it. Still wearing it, he paced the hotel room for a bit as though he were trying to kill some time—or this awkward moment. I could tell he was thoughtfully considering his words, measuring what he might say. (The word *minefield* comes to mind.)

"Pammy, I'm so sorry. Over the past two weeks, I went to the store several times, but I just couldn't think of anything to get you."

I said nothing. I think I batted my eyes a few times, absorbing this confirmation of my suspicion. I silently recalled the first Valentine's Day after we were married. Long story short, my husband stopped off at the Thrifty store on the way home from work and picked up a box of Whitman's. The cheap chocolate. The cheap, waxy chocolate. The not-even-See's chocolate. And, I'm pretty sure (if I remember correctly), without a Hallmark card.

It should be noted that there *was* some discussion on that mid-1980s day about John's last-minute purchase. It's a topic we've revisited over the years.

In *this* moment, I had a decision to make, and I had to make it fast—before Amygdala[7] got involved.

Option 1: I could pout. Be a little brat. Turn this into *a thing*. Just as I did thirty-four years ago.

Option 2: I could put this into context. I could consider that I'm on an all-expenses-paid trip on a breathtaking Caribbean island, lapping up the luxury *because* John has worked so hard and so smart for so long—in part, because he loves me so much. He's earned many reward trips like this one from his company, and I get to go along for the ride.

Option 1 has a bullet point: I could consider the fact that, last Valentine's Day, *I* was the one who came up a little short. I gave him a card, sans an accompanying gift. He probably doesn't recall it because he doesn't have an elephant's memory about such things. I, on the other

---

7 "Amygdala hijack" is a term coined by Daniel Goldman in his book *Emotional Intelligence: Why It Can Matter More Than IQ* (New York: Bantam, 1995). He says that the amygdala (the part of your brain that's responsible for emotional reactions) gets hijacked, shutting off the neocortex (the part of your brain that's responsible for logic, conscious thought, and sensory perception) when we have an instant, consuming emotional response disproportionate to the actual stimulus. Whatever the event, it triggers some sort of emotional threat, and we are hijacked. Which means we're not really thinking all that clearly, and we react. Which sometimes makes a person (me specifically) bratty.

hand, even remember what I said to him in my defense. I brandished an authoritative yet unsubstantiated claim to offset my guilt using these words: "I'm pretty sure the makers of Valentine's Day intended for the holiday to be more about the man giving the woman a gift, whereas the woman is to reciprocate with a nice card. This is confirmed by the fact that the word wife has the same number of letters as, and looks very much like, the word gift. Husband has way more letters and looks NOTHING like gift. Everyone knows this."

About a month ago, I searched out my childhood scrapbook. It had been in the attic for years, and although it reemerged a little worse for the wear, it was a treasure trove of memorabilia. Carefully turning the oversized, cluttered pages, I found an old love note from my fifth-grade boyfriend, Danny H. I remembered the scenario quite clearly. I had been feeling insecure about Danny's feelings for me, and at recess I asked his best friend, Steven N., to ask Danny: *Are we okay? Do you still like me?*

Seated back at our wooden desks, Danny passed a note to the class-mate behind him, and he or she in turn passed it on down the row of desks until it finally reached me. (It takes a village.) Written in his messy boy-handwriting, it read, "I love you and I always well [sic]. Even if I don't act like it."

I breathed a sigh. *Ah, it was a twofold message: our relationship was indeed strong, and not only that, there was a promise of undying love.*

Looking at that note a few weeks ago, his words became so much more meaningful because of his grade-school insight: ". . . even if I don't act like it." Sure, it's optimal that if you love someone, you act like it. But the truth is, sometimes we fall short. We're imperfect people, so of course we don't love perfectly. Why, then, would we expect perfection?

My literary hero, Anne Lamott, has said, "Expectations are resent-ments just waiting to happen." Anne, you rock.

John and I are heading over to Negril later today, a place bursting in Rasta colors and reggae sound. We've been there once before, eleven years ago, during another President's Club trip. We'll go to Rick's Café again, where we'll dine for our Valentine's Day meal while watching the cliff divers.

The marriage commitment is a little like that. We jump off the cliff into the water. It's scary. It's precarious. If we don't do it perfectly (which we won't!), we'll get hurt. We may even drown. Then again, the water landing can be pretty exhilarating.

The dictionary says a *hallmark* is a typical characteristic or feature of a person or thing. When Bob Marley sings of "One Love," I think he's referring to the One Love Who Does It Perfectly. The hallmark of God is His perfect love. That's what we can expect.

Marley sings of giving thanks and praise to the Lord; if we do that, there's promise that we will be all right. In that order. So today, I've decided to not be a brat. I've decided to give thanks and praise to the Lord. So we can be all right.

Happy Valentine's Day, love.

PS: I had John's blessing to share this story.

I Know She Happened

It's 3:08 a.m., and I just woke up from a dream about my friend Stacie. But I don't remember the dream. As much as I try, I can't retrieve it. I only have the flash of her face and the knowledge that I received a little visit from her.

The anniversary of Stacie's passing is approaching. I missed her memorial service at Saddleback Church around this time last year because I was leading a trip to Guatemala, and I couldn't bail on that because people were depending on me. I also knew that's what Stacie would have wanted me to do. Stacie was not a bailer.

I remember blogging a couple of times about Stacie after she passed. I just checked, and here's what I wrote on March, 9, 2016, the morning after she died. The time stamp is 3:08 a.m. Along with this little piece, I posted a photo of a stack of beautiful, juicy (as she would have referred to them), scrumptious chocolate chip cookies. On her cancer diet she'd gone without for three years.

Grief
The word looks like it feels.
It's 3:08 in the a.m. Hours after she left this place.
She spent roughly forty-six years showing us how to do love. To eat cookies with abandon.
There are people I want to smack who say things like "She's in a better place." Yeah, I know that. Duh.

But I'm not. I'm still here. Feeling the hole she's left.
Just let me feel it.
I believe in a higher place. I do. I've had a hint, a minuscule, so-slight-it-can't-even-be-categorized taste of the chocolate chip in that big cookie. I know she's munching right now on the best, tasty treat. And that fact makes me okay. Sort of. Makes this part semi-sweet doable for me.
My eyes are swollen, my heart is broken, but I do know you're good. You were. You are now, more than my tastebud-heart can imagine.
Mack down, Stace.

♥ ♥ ♥

I miss her so much.

I want to remember the details of the dream I just had, but all I can see is the outline of her face. Still, I know it happened.

I don't understand why we remember some dreams, while some slip away upon waking. Now that I think of it, I don't understand why we remember some things in real life, and some things we forget. I'm puzzled at my distinct memory of something so utterly insignificant as buying new Melamine dinner plates at Mervyn's fifteen-plus years ago, yet I can't remember key details of my wedding day, or even some things about my two kids' births.

Still, I know the wedding and the babies happened.

In the piece above about Stacie, when I wrote, "I've had a hint, a minuscule, so-slight-it-can't-even-be-categorized taste of the chocolate chip in that big cookie," I was referring to a few God encounters I've had over the years, specifically through dreams. I described one like this the morning after, while on vacation in Cabo:

> *Went to sleep last night unaware of any worries, listening*
> *to waves. Had an epic, full-length-feature type of dream—*
> *a stressful, heart-wrenching plot and troubling subplots with*

final scene in complete chaos, ending in destruction. Before the "credits" rolled, I heard a voice calmly say, "Trust Me." At that instant, I had a full body/mind/soul understanding; I knew as never before that all worry is pointless, that He's got it. And then I awoke.

In my life I've had three dreams where I've experienced a force and a power and a spirit I cannot describe.[8] What I know for sure is that they were heavenly, and I mean that in the most real sense of the word. There simply are no adjectives for the beauty of the experiences, but I can tell you that they were peeks and tastes and touches of heaven. Each time one happened, I awoke with a mind-blowing, momentary clarity . . . but also a sadness because I could not stay there. My sadness dissipated, though, as I relished the knowledge that these moments were promises of more to come, and that one day, I won't have to leave them at all.

I thought these dreams were so magnificent, so life-changing, so unforgettable that they would sustain me in living as a new person. I've tried to write them down, just in case. But like I said, there are no words, so my writing stinks. Over time, they fade. They always have. They slip away a little more each day.

Still, I know they happened.

The details of some things too beautiful often fade. (Are they too lovely for this planet?) I have the silhouette, however—the faint memory. God also lets me have other things as reminders, placeholders of images too magnificent for this place.

Two months after Stacie passed, I blogged the following piece:

---

8 For more on these experiences, see the chapter titled "REI" in Pamela Capone, *I Punched Myself in the Eye: Stories of Self-Sabotage, Imperfection, and Perfect, Amazing Grace* (Amazon CreateSpace, 2015).

I think of Stacie.

I think of Stacie when I put my purse down on the floorboard of my car and cover it with a jacket. Once when I met her at the lake to go for a walk, she quipped, "Yeah, no one will ever think that's a purse under that jacket and steal it."

I think of Stacie when I overfill my plate. Once at a bridal shower, she saw my dish and asked, "Hungry much?"

I think of Stacie when I see certain emojis in the selection on my iPhone. There was one in particular that was our go-to. I won't say which.

I think of Stacie when I hear the word adequate. Not because she was. That's what she answered every single time I asked her how she was feeling, when she was very, very sick.

I think of Stacie when I hear someone with a generous, unbridled laugh.

I think of Stacie when Facebook reminds me that I have a memory "on this day" with her, when it reposts something she said to me or a photo we were in together.

I think of Stacie when I put my feet up on the back of a theater chair.

I think of Stacie when I see my Jesus Calling *book and I remember, in the final days, how she'd trace her finger along the lines on the page as she slowly struggled to read aloud.*

I think of Stacie when I eat scrambled eggs and avocado.

I think of Stacie on Mondays now that I don't make my way across La Paz, from my street over to hers.

I think of Stacie without any visible reminders at all.

I'm going to Guatemala again soon, and I will think of her there too.

This morning, for now, the little visit last night was a chocolate morsel in the juicy cookie, and that taste will hold me over.

Because knowing she happened is enough.

The One Who Got Away

From what I can tell, there is romance at Sunrise Senior Home for the memory-impaired. Among the eligible singles, it appears that a few couples have paired off—I'm guessing matrimony, and possibly even some hook-ups.

Since I'm a self-professed people watcher, I imagine the current stories and backstories. I wonder about the widows and widowers, plus the ones who've never married, or the ones who still pine for *the one who got away*.

Several times during my visit yesterday at the Thursday afternoon happy hour, someone's hearing aid kept going off like a shrill alarm. I hear a similar high-pitched sound from my dad's hearing aid, and then I see him adjust it. But yesterday, from my vantage point, it appeared no one else was hearing it or doing any adjusting.

The red-vested, Eugene Levy–lookalike ragtime pianist banged out tunes for over an hour, including Christmas carols and even "The Old Rugged Cross," admitting that most everything he plays still sounds like ragtime. The energetic, engaging piano man kept wiping sweat from his brow, saying how he doesn't need to go exercise after he spends the afternoon here. Before each number, in a classic singsong voice, he would introduce the song, often adding a bit of trivia about the piece he was about to play.

"And here's a little number called 'Bumble Bee Boogie.' Yes, folks, the li'l guy has a warm heart *and no stinger!*"

A woman, who I'm guessing is a wife, leaned into her husband, smiled, and said—not exactly whispering, "Just like you!"

He shot a look at her like, "Hey, what's that supposed to mean!?"

Comforting him, she says, "Because you don't hurt me." And then they cuddled.

After the final song, I rolled Inez's walker to her so she could make her way over to her spot at the dinner table. Then I bent down and gave her a smooch on her cheek and a hug. I said I'd see her soon. I walked around the corner and to the door.

As I exited, a shrill alarm sounded, and I realized that what I'd thought was a rogue hearing aid was actually an alert for a resident who might be trying to make a quick dash. Perhaps this alarm is set during happy hour, when the sun is setting at Sunrise, and there is music in the air. Maybe those old melodies trigger some not-so-faded memories—and inspire a longing for that lost love, the one who got away.

Open a Can

Portland is a foodie mecca, and I make it a point to fit as many meals into a day as possible whenever I visit my daughter's city.

At the downtown Grilled Cheese Grill food truck, it's a sunny afternoon, 4:30 p.m.

As I'm standing near the truck, enjoying my pre-dinner sandwich, The Hot Brie (which I personally think should be named "Unbrierievable"), a hulking, twentysomething guy appears at my left, presumably waiting for his grilled cheese. I see that he's staring at my feet. "What kind of shoes are those? Like, are they for hiking?"

I look down at my feet, still chewing. "Yeah, well, I just use 'em for everyday walking around, but you could probably hike in them."

"So they're for hiking?"

"Yeah, you could probably hike in them."

"What brand are they?"

I finish swallowing the cheese-bread in my mouth. "They're Keens."

"So what size are they?"

"Um, these are 7½, I think."

He reaches down, runs his finger over them, brushes my bare heel. "I think that's a really common size for women."

"Okay, enjoy your sandwich." I skedaddle. (I think maybe he had what one would call a "feetish.")

There used to be a series of AT&T telephone commercials with the slogan "Reach out and touch someone." I don't think the kind of reaching out at the food truck was exactly what they were talking about though.

The Motown song "Reach Out and Touch"[9] (originally recorded by Diana Ross) speaks of reaching out for someone else's hand (*ahem*, not their feet). By doing so, says Ms. Ross, we can make this world a better place. Later, the song mentions something about seeing a down-and-out *friend on the street* and remembering that *his shoes could fit your feet*, so maybe that's where my Unbriereivable buddy got his idea, I don't know.

But that part about taking the opportunity to show kindness—that we can change things if we're proactive? Spot on, I think. Ross claims it comes *very naturally*, but I might disagree with that line. I think reaching out is actually a stretch, literally and figuratively—for all of us *sometimes*, and for some of us, *on the regular*. Not everyone is a touchy-feely type, even if in their heart of hearts they want to be. I've known people who are uncomfortable with physical affection, and you can sense their rigid discomfort right alongside their silent wanting-it-to-be-easy.

For all of us, sometimes the reaching part *can* be tricky. It's often scary because it may be uncharted—or perhaps damaged—territory.

Once the fear has been conquered and the "hand" has been out-stretched, I think the kindness itself can be as basic as a grilled cheese sandwich. It doesn't have to be fancy. In fact, simpler can be better. The "less is more" thing.

When I was little and I had a cold, my mom would *cook* (or so I thought) a bowl of Campbell's Tomato Soup and a grilled American cheese sandwich for me. When I got older, I understood the soup recipe: she just opened a can, added some tap water to a pan, and heated the

9 "Reach Out and Touch (Someone's Hand)," words and music by Nickolas Ashford and Valerie Simpson (Motown Records, 1970).

contents on the stove. I also realized—later—that there were other, tastier cheeses than American, like Brie. But when I have a cold as an adult, I reach back to my mom's comfort-food remedy: I remove the plastic from the waxy cheese, get out the bread, and open a can of soup.

People are walking around all over the place in different-style shoes, just needing a touch, some comfort. Whether it's easy or not, remove the plastic. Prepare some bread. Open a can. Respect boundaries. But do try to reach out to someone.

Perfect Moment

I don't say it very much, but every once in a while I admit, "I'm having a perfect moment." I don't say it much because, honestly, perfect moments are rare. I've been on this earth over half a century, so I've racked up a lot of moments—great moments, average moments, stinky moments, horrible moments, blah moments, indescribably most excellent moments, and once in a great while, a "perfect" moment. The perfect ones show up way less than the rest.

Exhibit A: surfing. I've only surfed a few times, mostly because it's really, really hard. And because it's also really hard. (I do love watching surfers, though. They are poetry in motion.)

In order to catch a wave, the planets have to align . . . not to mention so many other things that must come together in perfect synchronicity. You have to successfully navigate around other surfers, spot a rideable wave, properly anticipate the speed of the wave, paddle your arms like crazy and get into the wave's sweet spot, pop up on your board in time, stand on the right part of the board and balance so as not to do a liquid face plant. Plus, you must learn surfer lingo and eat an entire Pedro's burrito afterward. And those are just the initial instructions.

In other words, odds are really not great for catching a wave, especially for someone like me who's a lazy paddler and doesn't appreciate saltwater in her eyes. But on the rare occasion it's worked, it's been a little bit of heaven—the closest thing to walking on water.

There's another moment in my life that I classify as pretty much *perfect*, and it wasn't surfing, but it *was* on water. If Stacie hadn't been sick, it would have been most perfect.

It was May 2, 2015, and I was with some of my beloveds on a sailboat—my husband, John, my friend Debbie, and our friends Darren and Stacie. We were three miles or so offshore, Dana Point, California.

At that point, Stacie and Darren had been battling her brain cancer for over two years. I really don't have an adequate word for how valiantly they fought. While they fought, though, they did things such as going sailing. In Stacie's final days here, they strolled the sidewalks around that same harbor, and sometimes I got to join them. Stacie would be all wrapped up in a snuggly blanket, her legs tucked in, while her captain piloted her wheelchair.

But on that near-perfect day in May when she was a little less sick, we had already been having a pretty sweet time when our thirty-two-foot sloop called *Silver Moon* was suddenly engulfed by a pod of dolphins. As far as we could see, the lustrous, glorious party-crashers joined us for a ride-along, a play-along. For about fifty yards on either side of us and at least a mile ahead and behind us, possibly a thousand or more dolphins were performing a mesmerizing, impeccably synchronized swimming routine for free. For us.

John piloted the boat while Debbie, Stacie, and I watched the show from our front-row seats on the bow. I was sandwiched between my two girlfriends like a cheese panini at a perfect picnic.

Our enchanting ocean companions played and surfed and sailed, and their graceful movements took our breath away. And then, as if they had collectively agreed, "Our work here is done. Let's go," they redirected and swam off to other parts of the ocean, though all we heard was *eEeEeEeEeEeEeEeEeEeEeE* in their sweet dolphin language. In the video, I can hear Stacie saying, "Those guys are leaving us," as she laughs her easy, accepting laugh.

The dolphins stayed for a while on that day, and then they swam away. Darren had grabbed the camera and caught some of the show, but the video only captures a taste of the glory, like many things here below.

Stacie stayed for a while longer, and then her work here was done too. And then she had to go, moving on to the glorious unfathomable, which holds nothing but perfect moments.

Rebel without a Name Tag

I hate name tags. I'll put one on at an event if I must, though if I do, it will eventually, *accidentally on purpose* fall off (faulty adhesive or . . . whatever). While I typically am pretty good at understanding why I feel a certain way, I don't know why I loathe the tag. Maybe it feels like I'm walking around with a packaging label.

I do see the point, though. Especially when I'm at a function where I should remember someone's name and I do not. It's super helpful to be able to glance at that tag so as to avoid any awkward, "Heyyyyyy . . . how you doin'?" I like it when *other* people have name tags, for sure. That part works for me.

My mom only has the three of us kids—Cheryl, Danny, and me—but she almost never calls us by the correct name. This has been the case for long as I can remember, so it's not a "getting older" thing. At age eighty-nine, she's still sharp as a safety pin. But our names? Always a hangup. Most times she'll string every name together until she gets to mine, if she ever does. And I always answer to any of the names, including my dad's. I can just tell by her intonation when she means me. I don't know how else to explain it. From the other room, I'll hear her call, "Joe Cheryl Danny Pam . . ." Or sometimes it's just one of the names, like my dad's: "Joe!"

"Yes, Mom?"

I'm getting ready to take my yearly Guatemala trip where I'll go visit well over one hundred little girls, each having what feels like a hundred names. I've been making this pilgrimage at least once a year since 2008, and so I've seen many girls progress from kindergarten to graduation. I know lots of first names, and because I keep track of who's in school by their individual student ID, I'll sometimes see someone's three-digit number and their sweet face will flash in my mind as I'm doing my online IMA computer work here in the States.

On my first trip to IMA (International Medical Assistance) ten years ago, I couldn't sleep. Everyone else was napping at the missionary house just beyond one of the campus's walls, and although I tried, "nap" wasn't happening. Our red-eye flight from Southern California had landed in Guatemala City before sunrise, and all of my fellow travelers (who'd done this before) were trying to catch up on the sleep they'd missed. I was the rookie.

Fueled by either adrenaline or the TACA Airlines coffee, I was so amped about visiting the girls that I had walked the few steps over to the school in the early afternoon, entered the cafeteria through the back door, and peeked out the glass window to the courtyard playground, which is surrounded by classrooms. The only student I saw, however, was a lone girl walking from the restroom back to her class. Deflated, I figured I'd have to wait until recess.

I returned to the missionary house and unpacked. Then I walked back over to the cafeteria and checked the courtyard for signs of life. Still nothing. Back in my room, though, right about half past three, I heard the distinct sounds of children's laughter over the towering cinder-block wall. There were shrieks of joy, the ping of playground equipment, of recess time!

I bolted through the cafeteria and to the window, where I saw a sea of uniforms through a thin layer of playground dust. These were the IMA girls I'd heard so much about for so many years! As I slowly opened the glass door to step out into the playground, it seemed every student's head—every head that only a moment before was busy playing—stopped, turned, and looked to see who was there.

In an instant, hundreds of beautiful brown eyes were on me. And then, as though there was a unified, silent decision to swarm me, I was engulfed by little girls in crisp blue and red and white uniforms. With pleading, love-filled eyes, they embraced me, grabbed my hands, and wanted to know me.

So this is the IMA love I've been hearing about.

I sank to my haunches to meet them at eye level and try to communicate with them. Quickly frustrated, I couldn't understand a word—and this after months of Rosetta Stone Spanish. Then it occurred to me; I was hearing one sentence over and over again: *"Como se llama?"* I knew this question! Rosetta did not fail me!

I shot back: "My name is Pam!"

I heard giggles. "Bam?" They seemed confused and yet entertained by this strange American name. "Bam?"

I enunciated. "No, not Bam. Pam. *Pppp. Pppp.* Pam."

A chorus of "Bam?" continued. I gave up and decided to ask them their names.

I heard willing shouts of "Maria," "Lesli," "Angelica," "Joselin," "Lourdes," "Gabriela"—so many that I wished they had name tags to help me remember. Finally, I noticed a student standing demurely, silently sandwiched between the others and me, holding tightly onto my arm. Our eyes connected and I inquired, *"Como se llama?"*

She whispered, "Pamela."

I wasn't sure I'd heard her right. "Pamela? *Your* name is *Pamela?*"

She nodded rapidly, anticipating.

I yelped, *"My* name is Pamela!"

Her eyes widened. She seemed about to burst.

We embraced dramatically as though we were long-lost cousins who hadn't seen one another in years. Meanwhile, it registered with the rest of the girls that my name was indeed Pamela, and for some reason, so much easier to say than Pam.

We all laughed together at this beautiful start to what would be a profoundly moving week together at the IMA School—and years of ongoing friendship with little girls whose names I would come to know by heart.

After recess I checked the student roster, looking to see if Pamela was sponsored. She wasn't. Before school was over that day, I found her again and, with the aid of a translator, asked Pamela if she'd be okay with me sponsoring her. Her big, beautiful eyes smiling, she quickly nodded and melted into me. We were destined to be.

That moment is etched on my heart, as are my Guatemala girls.

They are not a student ID number. I'm not a number either. Thankfully, the God we share doesn't need to glance down and look at our name tags. He knows each of us by name.

Bedhead

It's Friday, and I've been in Guatemala since last Sunday. I haven't washed my hair yet, and it's so dirty I could form it into a topiary. This is fine because not only would I look good at Disneyland or fit right into the *Edward Scissorhands* film, but it makes bedhead even more fantastic, simply because it's malleable.

I *love* bedhead. It just makes a person so vulnerable, so endearing, so real. Real is good. I love seeing people on the street looking very . . . themselves.

This morning as I did my cardio on the road to IMA, I passed by many people with bedhead. This was perfect because we matched. Matching this way is good—we can be a little bit messy together. Plus, bedhead is a universal language. No matter the country, no matter the tongue, our bedheads communicate with one another. We all wake up, and we know at a glance that we're all a little sleepy still.

I'm a big fan of universal languages—and there are many. Here's just the tip of the topiary:

A smile.

A sad face.

Laughter.

Crying.

Kisses.

Art.

Sunrises.

Music.

A friendly wave.

Hugs.

An open heart.

Love.

Traveling recently to Jamaica, I noticed a custom that's also practiced in Mexico. When passing by a local, especially in the service industry, the other locals stop in their tracks and put their open hand to their heart. I find this to be quite beautiful. I may start doing this to get it going in the States. Join me?

The other evening, our team (visiting from the States) walked a few IMA students home in the village surrounding the school. There we met a student's *abuela*. As the grandma spoke, I noticed her hand on her heart. Even if she hadn't done this, I would have known this was the place from whence she was speaking. I heard and saw her gratitude for the IMA school and the impact it's had on her *nieta*—her granddaughter—their home, and their life. She would take her hand from her heart occasionally and then point it to the heavens, and although I could not understand *Español*, I understood she was thanking God for her abundant blessings. I understood her tears, and I'm quite certain she understood ours.

Another of my favorite universal languages is guilelessness. It's spoken with that thankful inflection in a voice, or the sparkle in an eye that glistens with a tear, or the hand on a heart that also points upward. It's spoken by those who cannot fathom putting on airs, who will open a heart before strangers and risk being known.

Not everyone lets themselves be malleable. But for those who do, it doesn't take long to discover how much we match. And in that moment, hearts instantly form into bonds—no longer strangers but trusted *amigos*, *hermanas*, friends, and sisters.

The Original Front-Porch Rocker

In the foreground of an old black-and-white photo, my grandpa Pete is standing in the dirt, his arms folded, leaning on a shovel, relaxed. On his head, a newsboy cap; on his face, wire-rimmed glasses and a humble confidence, a matter-of-factness. In the background is a sawhorse and what looks to be wooden boxes—maybe chicken coops—plus a plow, a leaning stack of tall wooden stakes, and possibly some cinder blocks. None of it looks like top-quality Home Depot materials, but apparently they used what they had.

Behind and to the right of this cluster of supplies is a white clapboard house, and standing on the porch is a woman in a housedress. This is my grandma Josephine. Her left hand is on her hip and her right arm's outstretched, leaning against the post. She has attitude and you can see it. Even though it's difficult to make out the expression on her face, *she knows who she is*, and she's as relaxed as Grandpa Pete, but with a little swag in her lean. To her left, at the bottom of the porch steps, is a chill, blonde ragamuffin sitting on the hood of a car.

Say what you want about what this classic photo might imply: a woman at home, a man in the field; or a woman standing behind her man. Some might call it a repressive, regressive, Tammy Wynette, "Stand by Your Man" scene—the traditional, man-doing-things-woman-doesn't-understand depiction. I don't see that in this picture. Grandma understood plenty. She was powerful.

Instead I see a snapshot of an expanding yet satisfied *home*. My mom speaks in such rich, glowing terms about what it was like growing up in this gentle Genaro household. She's said to me many times that "Pop never raised his voice."

I see the shovel in the photo as a focal point. The term *shovel-ready* is used to describe construction projects (usually large-scale infrastructure work) where planning and engineering are far enough along that, with adequate funding, construction can begin. The planning and engineering for Grandma and Grandpa's family "construction project" began in Italy, 1912. Married a short while, Grandpa left the old country and came to America solo to make sure he could get work and establish a safe landing spot for his wife and young son, Victor. After settling in, he sent for his little family.

Their eventual large-scale infrastructure (seven children) was built of mutual respect, self-respect, dirt-under-their-fingernails hard work, resolve, honor, the value of their word—and in a word, commitment. They were "funded" by a strong moral legacy handed down to them, and by an abundance of love, both earthly and above. They used what they had; they stood their ground; they dug in.

When they got older, my grandma and grandpa lived with us in California. I saw their sweet strength, and the fact that *they stood behind each other and next to one another*. Neither was less-than.

After my grandpa had a stroke, my parents set up a hospital bed smack-dab in the middle of our front den—in the center of our home, our living space. My mom added a respectful curtain partition allowing for privacy. I recall my grandma, always in a housedress, sitting by Grandpa Pete's hospital bed in her armchair. She seemed constantly relaxed, comfortable in her skin.

Once Grandpa passed away, I remember Grandma sitting in that same chair watching her two shows: *The Price Is Right* and *Let's Make a Deal*, only she called the former one *Bob Barker*. She didn't speak anything but Italian, but she nailed his name.

I have a memory of being in the den with her when a Vegas show-girl or a Radio City Rockette came on the TV screen. I can't recall the context, and maybe it was just a commercial, but the young woman was definitely showing some leg. Grandma said nothing. She just walked out of the room, still looking relaxed. She wasn't being holier-than-thou; she just knew who *she* was.

Now, I may be old-fashioned by many standards, but I still think I could stand to be a little more like Grandma, because I sit too much. Not physically, but in the way that counts.

Call me a prude if you want, but the debauchery I witnessed on Bourbon Street on a recent visit to New Orleans made me tear up. The activities some people classify under the guise of "freedom" or "fun" broke my heart. As I walked down that street, I actually thought of my grandma sitting in that chair and then walking out of the room.

Background or foreground, Grandma Josephine's humble confidence impressed upon me many things: when to stand, when to walk, when to stay and help lay the quality framework of a home on a solid foundation.

Grandma, you sure knew how to rock a front porch—and a legacy.

South of the Hoarder

Earlier today, while emptying my luggage, I stared at my cram-packed closet, knowing it was about to get crammier. I tried to jam shoes in any available crevice.

I felt a thought bubble start to, well, bubble as I imagined how nice it would be to have a walk-in closet. I thought of other women who have such closets and remembered those I'd heard say they use that space for praying. Bible teacher Priscilla Shirer calls it her "war room" because it's there that she gets on her knees and prays hard for those she loves—she goes to battle for them against the darkness of this world. Others too, like my sister Beth. I know she prays in her walk-in closet. A lot.

As I sat on the floor wedging shoes into nearly imaginary spaces, John walked into the bedroom. I motioned to the window sort of matter of factly. "You know, John, maybe we could push out this wall and make a nice walk-in closet. I know women who use their closets for prayer. I could be a *whole* lot more spiritual if I had a walk-in closet."

He laughed, *as he does*, and then walked out of the room.

I glared at my closet with the volcano of shoes I haven't worn in forever (but keep for *just in case*) and the clothes hanging so tightly I couldn't fit another hanger, and I considered the alternatives until, you know, we renovate and I can get *my* war room.

So I can be more spiritual.

I pondered putting a Tuff Shed of sorts somewhere inside or outside the house, for the out-of-season and out-of-size *just in cases* that I might still need. Then I thought of a quote I'd read just *yesterday* by Socrates. Yesterday.

"He is nearest to God who needs the fewest of things."

The timing seemed interesting, albeit a little obnoxious.

By "things," I suspect Socrates meant the material and the immaterial. The material, of course, includes dusty (literally dusty) shoes and too-tight jeans and additional storage rooms needed to house those items. The immaterial might be stuff like unmet expectations from relationships and not-yet-attained dreams. The lists, both material and immaterial, are practically endless. Well, mine are.

A book I read many years ago, maybe back in the 1980s, was simply titled *Simplify*. I'd lost track of it and gone searching for it at one point, but couldn't find it. And then I remembered giving it away because of my newly formed, reduce-reuse-recycle mind-set, *courtesy of the book*. It was the perfect application of the writer's message. I felt noble. Untethered. After reading it, I'd gutted our family condo of excess stuff. Streamlined our abode.

The book transformed my life. For a minute. Thinking maybe I needed a revisit today, I Googled the title. Maybe I'd buy it again.

Ironically, on Amazon alone, there were *twenty* pages of books on the notion of minimalism—simplifying, de-cluttering, downsizing, making space, living with less, the joy of less. With so many books to read on the subject, how can they all have a different spin on the idea of *simplify*? Isn't it supposed to be . . . simple?

I remember once, also many years ago, reading a very large book in public. The tome was as hefty as The Bible or *Moby Dick* or *War and Peace*. At the time, I had taken up running and was serious about it, completing ten miles a day. This book was the bible of running books, and so I felt official. On the bright-red cover in big, white lettering it read: *Running*. Below that was a profile of two muscled legs in motion, equipped with red Onitsuka Tiger running shoes.

A passerby observed, "Why do you need a book about running? Don't you just run?"

I didn't answer him but gave him the side-eye. I didn't know the answer. It just seemed that if I was a runner and someone wrote a very large book about running, I should probably read it.

Sitting on my bedroom floor in front of my warring closet of chaos today, my instinct was to add rather than subtract. *Gimme, gimme, gimme* instead of *Clear out, make space, and embrace the glorious void.*

I'm not that bad, really. Imagine a hoarder diagram and the phrase "Average hoarder" is dead-center, and then above that is "Extreme hoarder," and above that is "Reality TV show hoarder." Below "Average hoarder" is "Mild hoarder," and below that is just "Hoarder," which is barely *hinting* at hoarding. Technically, I would fall somewhere below that. Way south of the Hoarder.

By all appearances, my house does not look like a hoarder has taken up residence. At least, not until you peek in my drawers, look up in the attic, or slide open my closets. (I hope that's not a metaphor.)

If memory serves, I was on a claw-foot tub campaign for YEARS. I essentially told John that my life would be perfect if I could have a free-standing claw-foot tub. *Perfect.* I'd always wanted one, and life felt a little *off* without one. If I had one, *ahhhhh,* I could soak; I could relax, washing away the chaos while inspiration bubbled up; I could pray.

I finally got the tub a couple of years ago. And my life's not perfect. Sometimes there's chaos. I don't take nearly enough bubble baths either.

If memory continues to serve, years before that, right after we'd moved into our current home, I'd campaigned hard to have the hill on our backyard terraced into a real-live, functioning garden (tomatoes are so romantic, Italian, and peaceful!) leading to a secret garden at the top, hidden among the wooded brush. How idyllic it would be to have a sitting space up there—me, alone in "the wild," enjoying a private outdoor nook where I could read and write and pray. My life would have so much serenity. I'd be so spiritual.

I hardly go up there.

You know where I'm headed with this . . . I don't need a bigger closet. I don't need a special tub. I don't need a place in my pretend woods. I need to throw away crap.

"He is nearest to God who needs the fewest of things."

I know I'm not alone in this. America is covered in storage facilities. Covered.

My overthinking, my overneeding, my overcomplicating is *my* war room, but not in the productive, Priscilla Shirer kind of way. It's the counterproductive, warring-within-oneself way. My tendency for delay and detour, distractedness, and diversion is what causes me to miss the forest for the trees on my lush backyard hill.

The answer is indeed simple. The very thing I desire—the stillness, the quiet—is available any time, any place, at any moment. I could be a *whole* lot more spiritual if I needed a little less to get there.

Peace is within my reach. I don't need a thing.

Strangers in the Car Wash

Standing at the floor-to-ceiling window, I watch my slippery, red, driverless MINI Cooper inching by, smoothly transitioning from huge sudsy brushes and cloths. A man walks up, stands by my side, stares at my gliding MINI, and speaks. I do not know him, and there's no one else around.

Him: "If you have thyroid cancer, should you have your thyroid removed?"

I look on my other side, confirming he's talking to me. I look back at him. I do a mini shrug.

Me: "Um, I don't know."

Him: "Do you know about other cancers?"

Me: "No, not so much."

Him: "Do you have your thyroid?"

Me: "Yes, I believe I do." (I wanted to snidely say, "Last time I checked.")

Him: "Do you drink canyon water?"

Me: "No." (Here's where I get busy looking at my iPhone.)

Him: "Everybody's on their cell phone. That's all people care about. No one talks to people about God."

Me: "I talk to people about God on my cell phone."

Him: "You do?"

Me: "Yeah, sometimes."

Him: "Do you wanna buy a Honda?"

Whoa, way to transition, buddy. Ever hear of a segue?

Dude came at me ready to dialogue, no doubt about that. I can respect that. We hadn't met yet, but that doesn't mean we were strangers. I mean, who decided "stranger" was a good way to describe the Unmet?

I concur with Yeats that there are no strangers here on this big, round earth, only friends we haven't yet had the pleasure of meeting. Think about some of your relationships. Weren't at least some of them a result of being open to having a conversation with an Unmet? Maybe even your significant other.

Our lives can change in a moment. We're open and the world opens up, up. Down the road, that person could end up being someone you couldn't imagine life without.

I'm not always willing to have a conversation. Sometimes you have to set what's called a *conversation expectation*. Like on a plane, for example. On more than one occasion, I've engaged in a conversation with a seat partner early on, and then we *had* to talk the entire fifteen-thousand-hour flight. What I'd like to know is, how do you turn your head to that person, smile, and politely say, "You know what? I'm done. You're nice and all, but I don't want to talk any more. Not one more word"? (I'm even inclined to put my thumb and index fingers together at my lips as if I'm locking them up, followed by the over-my-shoulder key toss.)

But you simply can't be that brazen. I've tried. So if you say anything more than a simple greeting, consider yourself committed for the entire flight.

Here's the other downside: it's not pleasant for the neighbors. I was on a flight a couple of weeks ago where I was seated across the aisle from a Chatty Cathy and a Talkative Tom, and I wanted to flip the beverage cart over on their heads.

There's such a thing as too much of a good thing, people! Be cordial, but draw the line. Some people don't want to listen to your four-hour conversation about your trip Down Under and why it's so hard to get a toddler to take a nap. A greeting is more than sufficient. A smile with a nod is fine. Beyond that, you're signing your own death warrant.

Outside of air travel, though, I encourage conversations with the Unmet.

Once, on vacation, I had a massage where the therapist flat-out spoke truth into my life. We got into some very serious topics in the space of fifty minutes while I stared at the ground, naked, my face hung through a hole. Her words were absorbed into my heart like the massage oil into my skin.

I'm not a fan of small talk. It's the reason I don't love parties. That herky-jerky moving from person to person and doing a five-minute recap of what's-new, what-do-you-do? No thanks. I'd rather be the host of the party, where I can be distracted, gliding through the kitchen, hovering above the idle chatter, feeding and hydrating the masses. Or if I *have* to be a guest, pair me in a corner with a big talker who wants to dialogue about the juicy stuff. The things that matter on earth and above.

There's a reason it's called *small* talk. It's puny. Give me the meat. *That's* the life of the party.

Take Forrest Gump, for example. He was a big talker, believe it or not. And the Unmet were his peeps. In the opening scene of *Forrest Gump*, we see a crew-cut, Sunday-best with well-worn sneakers Forrest sitting on a bench, a slim white box on his lap as he apparently waits for the city bus. A woman in a nurse's uniform walks up, sits down on the other end of the bench, and immediately pulls a *People* magazine out of her oversized purse. She promptly begins reading, clearly setting a *conversation expectation*.

Forrest looks to his right and says, "Hello, my name's Forrest. Forrest Gump."

She does the acknowledgment nod.

Forrest opens the box, offers her a chocolate. She shakes her head, *no thank you*. He brings the box back to his lap. "I could eat about a million and a half of these," he says.

No response.

"My momma always said life is like a box of chocolates." He takes a bite of one of the candies, and with a full mouth continues: "You never know what you're gonna get."

Forrest closes the box, looks down, and points to the woman's shoes, not that dissimilar from the way the Grilled Cheese Grill Dude pointed to (and in my case, touched) mine. There's something very *relating* about shoes, it seems. Universal, grounding.

Forrest says, "Those must be comfortable shoes. I bet you could walk all day in shoes like that and not feel a thing." He looks down at his own shoes. "I wish I had shoes like that."

The nurse finally speaks, to enlighten him to her reality. "My feet hurt."

"Momma always said, there's an awful lot you can tell about a person by their shoes. Where they go. Where they've been."

The nurse now turns her head to him; she's listening intently. She recognizes *big talk*. There's a long pause. He's thinking.

"I've worn lots of shoes," he reflects. "I bet if I think about it real hard, I could remember my first pair of shoes."

He scrunches up his face, concentrating harder. "Momma said they'd take me anywhere . . ."

If you think about it, Forrest segues from small to big in under a minute because, from the start, his small talk *is* big talk. It's all metaphor. It's all about life experience—generosity, honesty, openness, expectations, assumptions, relating to others' journey, personal desires, fate, serendipity, childhood memories, life roles, adventure, unlimited potential—things that matter both on earth and above.

There's a line in the seventies song "Car Wash" by Rose Royce: "There ain't no tellin' who you might meet."[10] Be open to random acts of conversation with the Unmet. You just never know whose path you're gonna cross and what good things you're gonna get.

---

10 "Car Wash," music and lyrics by Norman Whitfield (MCA, 1976).

Sunblock

Rick's Café is one of *the* hoppin' hot spots in Negril, Jamaica, and we totally scored on this corner table. Not only could we watch the fearless acrobatic cliff jumpers, but we were front and center for what was shaping up to be a jaw-dropping sundown.

It always does my heart good to see so many people who still value a good sunset—that the novelty's never worn off. On a sandy beach, on a boat, in the mountains, at a restaurant such as Rick's, and once, even over a Bakersfield concrete overpass, it's like, *Hey, the human race hasn't gotten so far off the rails that we don't still love those moments that build toward a masterpiece.* We haven't been so jaded by political rhetoric and terrorism and materialism that we can't come together and appreciate the glorious mural in the sky. The pure miracle that we had absolutely nothing to do with and can take no credit for.

Collectively and individually, we see it coming together. It's like God is up there with His colorful palette in one hand, a paintbrush in the other, wearing a pure white beret and a flowing smock with gold threading. He steps back and speaks under His breath, *Okay, yeah, I think I'll pull in some darker tones in this cloud over there; contrast that one with this white, puffy, almost-translucent one just below; add a silvery one up top . . . Yes, this is going to blend nicely with the golden fireball dropping into the ocean. You're going to love this one tonight, guys . . . I can't wait to see your faces. If this doesn't convince you of Me . . ."*

From our vantage point at Rick's, I could see a sailboat starting from the far left edge of this evening's canvas, and if the timing was right, its tiny, pearlescent sails would be a brilliantly illuminated triangle, a little extra somethin'-for-your-trouble, in the center of the Caribbean vista as the sun slipped past the ocean's edge.

I observed the other diners as twilight closed in: people doing lone selfies, couples doing duo selfies, families asking a kind stranger, *Would you mind snapping our photo?* Small groups and large groups were all vying for the same corner of Rick's deck—right in front of *our* table and *our* view of the burgeoning sunset.

The optical illusion of the sun picking up the pace right at the end of its daily descent sends tourists scurrying to stand in *just* the right spot. They *want* this. People take turns, some edging others out with their pearly, Crest Whitestrip smiles. The massive group organizes themselves, readying their phones and cameras for the perfect moment when the sun meets the sea.

From where I sit, I have the perfect view of what one group photographer will be capturing. And it will *not* be the anticipated crescendo, for the expanse of their group is completely blocking the object of everyone's desire. Including ours.

There will be no pièce de résistance in their photo. Or in our eyeline. *Thanks.*

On this evening, John and I had the perfect table, and yet we would miss the perfect view.

Sometimes we humans miss the boat. We scurry around into position, relying on our own efforts to obtain an objective, when really, all we had to do was . . . get out of our own way.

Tour-Bus People

I love movies—I am transported by a good story. Maybe because the Oscars celebrate movies, I love watching the Oscars too. One year, when I poorly timed my Guatemala trip, I found the show live on a Guatemalan station but ended up watching the fuzzy broadcast with a ten-second delay, dubbed in Spanish. It was confusing, to say the least. Still, I muddled through.

While I thought host Jimmy Kimmel did a great job last night at the eighty-ninth Academy Awards, the show for some reason felt a little ho-hum until the moment we'd all been waiting for, the award for Best Picture. In case you missed it, the *wrong* film was mistakenly announced as the winner, and after some very real, completely unscripted, deer-in-headlights glances across the stage, there was an "Oh, you know what? Never mind. It's not for you, it's for *them*" moment. As awkward and unfortunate as it was, the concluding chaos and confusion and drama sort of made up for what had preceded it.

Digesting the entire four hours, there were two elitist segments that stuck in my craw.

Segment One: I understand why, in theory, it may have been a funny gag to bring an unsuspecting tour-bus group from Hollywood Boulevard into the Dolby Theater while the Oscars were going on, but it felt a little . . . exploitive. Maybe that's a stretch, but something about watching the "little people meet the big people"—i.e., "the bumpkins meet the VIPs"—annoyed me. Without their permission, the tourists were paraded in front of the first row of A-listers like, *Oh, look how the shiny ones will stoop to say hello to the peasants!*

Segment Two: The Best Supporting Actress's acceptance speech. I won't name her in case she now has regret, but she actually said: "I became an artist, and thank God I did, because we are the only profession that celebrates what it means to live a life."

Sitting on the couch with John, I gasped. "What?!"

I could name a few other professions—other people—who are *not celebrated* yet who celebrate life *every single day*, not just while on a movie set. I want to give this actress the benefit of the doubt that she misspoke. But in case she meant it exactly the way it sounded, I have to say something about a few people I know, such as . . .

My cousin Lou, who volunteers his time, resources, and talent with an organization in Uganda that's digging wells for people who are dying of thirst. He's celebrating life.

My sister Beth, a retired first-grade teacher who now runs a pre-K out of her home free of charge to families. Life celebrating, right there.

Maryann, Shari, and Tina—three friends who had a vision for women in developing nations, and who began IMA. And Haydee, an IMA super-volunteer, who poured her life into the cause until she passed away. The IMA celebration continues.

Darlene, founder of HOINA (Home of the Indian Nations) orphanage, has been celebrating what life is like in South India since 1971.

Chemo Pals like my daughter, Cassie, who volunteer to come alongside a child who's scary-ill.

Daughters like my cousin Amaya who take care of and honor an aging parent.

Life-activist and volunteer extraordinaire Jeni in Napa, who has her finger in so many pies she could fill a bakery.

Tiffany, who puts little shoes on bare, little feet all over the world with Soles4Souls.

My cousin Amy, who holds an annual fundraiser for women who can not afford feminine products.

And Darren, who fought *every day* for his wife's life, that Stacie would live one day more.

The list of people and professions who celebrate what it means to live a life is endless. You could maybe call them tour-bus people. Unsung doctors and nurses and soldiers and cops and firefighters and pastors and teachers and moms and dads and foster parents and people with terminal illness who fight valiantly and daily to stay alive. Cancer researchers and the donors who fund research, such as my husband's former boss, Don. Obscure Mother Teresa–types all over the world who are touching and healing the forgotten . . .

I could go on, but I won't. Except to say: Reality check, Hollywood. Others celebrate what it means to live a life too.

Little Orphan Esther

What I love about the biblical story of Esther is that many of the key players are underdogs. They are also sometimes the defiant ones, the rabble-rousers, the movers and fist-shakers who will not go against who they are or what they believe.

The time and place is post-exile, fifth-century BC Persia, where a group of Jews has stayed behind after some of their cohorts have returned to Jerusalem.

The first system bucker is Vashti, the reigning queen of Persia. She doesn't get a lot of screen time, but to me, her short performance sets a tone and packs a wallop. Her misogynistic husband, the king, tries to treat her as a trophy at a palace party, and she's like, *Not on my bejeweled, royal watch, buddy. I'm no parade float.* Offended by Vashti's noncompliance, the king removes her crown, and she hands in her queen card. Exit stage left.

Enter orphan Esther, the young beauty who's been lovingly raised by her older cousin, Mordecai, a total firebrand underdog himself. Esther is enrolled in a pageant to replace ex-queen Vashti, but she keeps her Jewish heritage a secret for protection. Because ragamuffin Esther is a knockout, she wins the beauty contest. The king is smitten, and he places a sparkly crown on her head, declaring her the new queen.

Cousin Mordecai keeps tabs on his beloved cousin but eventually gets into hot water himself because, as a faithful Jew, he refuses to kneel before anyone but God (and in particular, refuses to worship the king's right hand, aka arrogant royal dude and villain in our story, Haman). Haman is so enraged by Mordecai's audacious, no-kneeling policy that he determines to wipe out *all* the Jews in the land. Thinking *That'll get 'em*, power-hungry Haman convinces the king—who is still unaware that his current arm candy is a Jew—to agree to the genocide.

This is when Mordecai suggests to Esther that she ought to play *her* queen card, come clean about her heritage, and try to persuade the king to change his mind about Haman's plan. Mordecai delicately balances things to his cousin by saying she doesn't *have* to do this; he knows that if she doesn't agree to it, God will still find a way, though maybe not in *their* time, and they both know what that means—it could produce a royal flush, right down the toilet, for all of them. Mordecai goes on to utter that famous, poetic line "for such a time as this," suggesting that perhaps this is the *very* reason she was named queen in the first place.

Esther knows the stakes and understands that, even though she's queen, approaching the king uninvited is a huge no-no and could put her on the stake. Nevertheless she says, "If I perish, I perish." Girl's got chutzpah.

The story of Esther includes some of my favorite themes and elements. There's a whole lot of big-picture seeing, all-in risk-taking, renegading, buying-the-farm, and self-sacrificing, plus plenty of *carpe diem*-ing amid flat-out faith, righteous defiance, tenacity, and "strategery." There are ironic reversals, comeuppances, delicious plot twists in favor of the good guys, and solid evidence that God does not abandon His people or His promises regardless of appearances or status or human schemes.

As a reader/watcher, I generally like a story that lets you do *just enough* work. One that doesn't leave you scratching your head because you're so lost, but one that doesn't insult your intelligence either, by precisely spelling things out.[11] One that, if you're paying attention, you see the subtleties, the nuances; you see the miracles taking place, God's behind-the-scenes handiwork. There's enough evidence to grow your faith, and yet you get the yummy satisfaction of sort of figuring out the faith connection yourself.

Example: In the entire book of Esther, God's name isn't mentioned even once. That fact alone could tempt a person to discredit its events as coincidence, mere happenstance. However, when you take all the facts into account, it's pretty tough to truly absorb the story without seeing Him in it. He's all over it. God is there even when He may appear to have bailed and you think you and your people might be doomed.

Still, there is space for your free will: You choose to believe. Or not. God doesn't fill in every blank. He doesn't want a robot or a slave; He wants our trust.

I see evidence in Esther's story (and many others in Scripture) that our faith carries a whole lot of weight with God—far more weight than our box-checking and rigid rule-keeping do. He cares about our dare.

As for me, it's sometimes more of a creep of faith than a step of faith. I tend to slink toward the scary edge, peeking over the side, measuring the depth of the plunge. My hope is that my faith gets stronger and bolder with experience—that I more often take a confident running start and catch a little air, looking to the far side of the deep crevasse rather than down into it, assured that my Redeemer, my Rescuer, waits on the other side of the scary chasm, ready to catch me with His arms open wide.

---

11 This is also the way I like to tell a story, and one of the reasons I hope you get just enough out of my little teaser that you will be intrigued to open the actual book of Esther for yourself.

Two Demure Girls at the Jazz Club

It was five minutes before 4 p.m., which is the dinner hour at Sunrise Senior Living, and the smooth jazz singer was wrapping up her set. During the last number, the residents do their version of the mad dash from their prime spots near the blond upright piano over to their favorite dinner chairs. Walkers and wheelchairs converge into something like the El Toro "Y," where the 405 and the 5 meet in Orange County, California.

My friend Inez and I happened to be stationed near the back of the dining area when the leg of my chair got stuck in the bottom portion of that freeway. A much older, stockier, balding Rhett Butler headed directly to our Y in his wheelchair. As he neared, he picked up speed. I could see his eyes on mine, and from a couple of yards away he began mouthing the words "You're a beautiful woman" right before he puckered his lips.

I wasn't sure if he *was* puckering up exactly—whether unintentionally (due to an involuntary condition that sometimes occurs in the elderly) or intentionally—but as he inched forward and I could hear what he was saying, it all became clear. Repeating the words, he leaned toward me as far as he could, raised his eyebrows, puckered his lips *hard*—like he meant it now, like he was Rhett to Scarlett, declaring, "You need kissing badly . . . that's what's wrong with you. You should be kissed, and often, by someone who knows how."

Even though this moment unfolded in a sort of surreal slow motion, I had a split-second decision to make. And I thought, *What the heck.*

I leaned into his wheelchair. His eyes got wider, his eyebrows higher, and like a heat-seeking missile, he shot straight for my lips. And I, as a demure Christian woman with respect for my husband and my vows, turned my cheek. Slightly.

He was visibly stunned. I think we all were.

I looked to my right, and Inez's eyes were impossibly wider than his, her mouth doing that little *O*, and then I heard a teeny "Oh my," followed by her demure, shoulder-shaking chuckle. We're both a little demure.

So that was my day: a man at Sunrise Senior Living—a residential home also known as "A Special Neighborhood for the Memory-Impaired"—planted one on me. I may have needed it as much as he did.

He has likely already forgotten it.

I never will.

Detour

We tend to be painfully dramatic here in Southern California when we get weather other than straight-up sunshine. If rare sprinkles are in the forecast, the local news immediately flips to the *dun dun dun* music with bold, flashing graphics—STORM WATCH [fill in the year]—with all kinds of apocalyptic-sounding tips on how to weather the weather. And pretty much all the time, those warnings turn out to be false alarms, and then meteorologists like Channel 7's Dallas Raines tuck their tail and are like, *Um, never mind.*

Personally, I was blindsided by the record-breaking deluge in California between late 2016 and early 2017. Maybe I just wasn't paying attention to the local forecasts, but I hadn't heard any advisories to hunker down for another El Nino (the last time we had any brag-worthy rain was 1997–98). This year, though, the rain just kept coming. And coming. Our "rainy season" resulted in at least sixty deaths and widespread property damage. That was the bad news. The good news? We had green here like I don't think I've ever seen. The spring colors exploded.

On days when I have more time, I'll throw my bike on the rack of my car and head to one of California's many mountain-bike trails. But if I only have an hour to ride, I hop on my bike at my house and take my go-to route: a paved path along our partially concrete, suburban creek bed called the Oso Trail. It's a decent view for suburbia, and a decent workout.

This year, with the mountain-bike trails saturated by the storms, I was going to my go-to a lot. Even *it* was a little worse for the wear over the weeks of hard precipitation—trees down and varying degrees of sliding mud and puddles and stick obstructions.

One day, about a third of the way on the Oso, I pedaled up to a road sign that stated in no uncertain terms that the next section of the trail was now impassable. Additional signs pointed to a detour. Apparently, my go-to would be out of commission for weeks.

I don't like detours. And of course, signs don't apply to me, so I rode around the barrier and went off-road, edging closer to the creek and to the very area I was warned against. I could see the machines and the construction workers in their reflective gear, and the men's faces were saying, *What are you doing? You can't be here. Can't you read the sign?* One guy in a hard hat began waving his arms and yelling for me to stop and go back. I waved him off, flashing my *I've got this; it'll be fine. You don't know my suburban creek skills* smile.

He emphatically shook his head at me and put his hand up, instantly transforming into a shades-wearing, mustached traffic cop. I finally relented, turned my bike around, and pedaled toward the detour and up a steep incline.

At the top of my detour, I found myself in a land I didn't realize existed: vibrant green baseball fields; a sun-drenched, towering, multi-colored children's play structure clamoring with giggling children; moms with strollers chatting with other moms chasing their climbers; lovely Adirondack chairs positioned in both the shade and the warm sun; benches and fountains and sculptures; mosaics, table chess set-ups, and a bocce ball court occupied by older men like I'd seen in my idyllic Italy. It was a heavenly park above the creek bed, and it had been here all along. I had no idea. I had no idea what I'd been missing.

Suddenly, I heard an impassioned male speaking in Spanish, using words like *espíritu* and *Jesu Cristo*. I saw the elderly man sitting on a park bench with his head bowed, a thick book on his left and a laptop in front of him. He was speaking into the computer as though he was being recorded. As I listened, I heard more familiar words in his Spanish tongue. He appeared to be preaching, or practicing preaching, and he was *belting* it out, giving all he had, as though he were a Hispanic Billy Graham standing on a stage in an arena before an audience of eighty thousand. I dismounted my bike and just stood and listened. I could hear the children's laughter in the background, the elderly man's voice booming over their playtime sounds.

I've been doing the detour for weeks since then, and I've seen the preacher man many times, always in the same spot, delivering his message. Each time I've stopped to listen, sneak a few photos, and embrace the moment.

Last week, I saw that the detour signs had been removed and that the work crew was gone. The path was repaired, and I could continue on my old route.

But I opted to take the detour.

I saw the preacher-man again, preaching into his laptop, book to his side. I got off my bike and walked over, smiled, said *Permiso*, and asked if he spoke English. He smiled, shook his head, and said a line I did not understand. So of course I kept talking, trying harder to enunciate my English. I asked if he was practicing a sermon. He smiled again and, I think, repeated what he had just said. My memory flashed back to the time I was seated next to a Guatemalan woman on a plane and she kept talking to me in Spanish even though I told her, "*No habla Española.*" Here, I was *that* woman. I told the preacher—still in English—that I loved listening to him, and I hoped it was okay. He just kept smiling.

I'm a creature of habit, no doubt about it. If I hadn't been forced to take a detour, I might never have experienced the park. Life's a little like that too. Sometimes when I think there's only one way I need to go, I am forced off my route and told to go another way (most times, a better way). I typically resist this change of direction. But when I embrace the detour, I experience a new and heavenly place where a good word is waiting.

A few days ago, I was in a traffic cram on the 5 Freeway in the heart of Los Angeles. This was an unfamiliar destination, so I was using the Google Maps app on my iPhone. A message popped up suggesting a better route, considering the jam. I've taken that option before and gotten lost, so I hesitated. Plus, I was in a pretty sketchy area of the city and wasn't sure it would be safe. So I sat there. For a while. And then the digital voice spoke up again.

While "parked" next to the off-ramp she was suggesting, I looked into my right rear view, saw no cars coming, and punched it. On the short, downward slope of the off-ramp, I could see the freeway *on-ramp* directly in front of me. Easy on, easy off. Then the Google Maps voice simultaneously told me to stop at the stop sign *and* get right back on the freeway . . . as if this detour was pointless. That's when I saw a woman standing at the off-ramp stop sign. She was holding a sign asking for help, her grocery cart full of belongings nearby—the signs of homelessness. I looked over to the passenger floorboard on my right and the gallon Zip-loc bag peeking out. On the side of it, written in black Sharpie, was "Love bag," one of the many such bags John and I had assembled as a love project. Among other things, it was filled with snacks, a toothbrush and toothpaste, fresh socks, a five-dollar bill, and an encouraging note I had written to ragamuffins just like me.

I grabbed the bag, rolled down my window, and as I neared the stop sign, I handed a little love to the woman. She peeked into the bag, brought it to her chest, and with a tone that matched her good word, she said, "Excellent." I immediately knew this was the very reason for this detour.

Juxtaposition

Right out of the chute, I will say I have been wildly blessed. I live a grateful life. What's also true is, like everyone else on the planet, I learned early on that life isn't fair.

Generally, I don't walk around disgruntled or surprised by the inequities. Saddened by them sometimes, yes; surprised, no. Facebook has given us a great big, blue platform where we can compare. I love what Anne Lamott has said about comparison, though: "Never compare your insides to someone else's outsides."

I travel regularly to Guatemala. I've been to Haiti. I've been to places not-so-distant where the struggle is very, very real for the people who live there. And while good versus evil is a basic story archetype, it's not hard to imagine the two realities running parallel in our lives. Still, there *have* been times that I've been surprised—no, *blindsided*—by the acute paradox that these realities exist simultaneously, sometimes as neighbors. A recent experience provided the most undeniably vivid depiction of this juxtaposition, and I am still processing it.

My husband, John, and I had just spent three days at Torre del Falco, a hilltop castle in Spoleto, Italy. We'd celebrated our thirty-third wedding anniversary and had the entire tower to ourselves. It was Umbrian heaven. We had loaded up our rented Yaris hybrid and were headed down the winding, unpaved road toward the autostrada (Italy's toll road) to begin our drive through the area's idyllic rolling hills and vineyards.

While we had never been on this specific stretch of highway, it was our fifth trip to Italy—my favorite place in the world—and I'd encountered scenery that took my breath away every time. (Note to travelers: There is one place in particular in San Gimignano, Tuscany, that has become my "happy place," the location I return to in my head when I need to relax my chaotic mind to pray or meditate. It's such an ethereal view, I made a poster-size print from a photo I'd taken, and it hangs above our claw-foot tub. I visit that actual spot on every trip because, since the first time I stood at the edge of the hill that overlooks the vineyards, it broke my heart in all the best ways.)

I didn't think anything could compare to that hilltop view in San Gimignano.

John and I had literally just departed the castle and started our descent down the curvy dirt road when my phone rang. I answered the call, and thus began one of the most disturbing conversations I've had in my life. I will not go into the details, but the call took me from a metaphorical and literal hilltop into a valley. As I felt the heaviest of darkness trying to infect my mind and break my heart in the worst way, I was physically surrounded by the most verdant, jaw-dropping beauty I had encountered, maybe even surpassing the view from that hillside in San Gimignano. Vineyard after vineyard, rolling hill after rolling hill, the uniform lines of vines were "perfectly staggered" the way an artist might paint a landscape, and dotted with variations of bursting, majestic colors. It was a crazy irony—an emotional, lethal toxin being forced down my throat as my eyes thirsted for the glory instead.

When we'd pass into the darkness of the mountain tunnels, I could see the small, lit circle of green at the end growing bigger and bigger until we were birthed out the other side, back into the full-scope brilliance. At one point, after about thirty minutes on the phone, I'd lost connection while we were in a tunnel. You might wonder why I didn't just end the phone call deliberately early on. The answer, simply: I was unable.

As I put my phone in my lap and became suddenly more aware of the nausea that had been building, I realized I had to vomit. I'd heard of people getting physically ill after upsetting news, but it had never happened to me before.

On the side of the SS77 toll road just outside of Foligno, John pulled to the narrow margin saved for emergency parking, and I opened the car door and began to wretch. My body wanted it *out of me*. As I hung my head with tears running down my face, I looked above and saw perhaps the greatest grandeur ever.

I was gobsmacked. And one word burst into my mind: *juxtaposition*.

While I continued to heave, I noticed that right next to me on the asphalt—literally less than six inches from my face—was a pile of human excrement, complete with wadded up toilet paper. (Yes, it is a necessary detail of this story.) Someone else had exited the tunnel and had to get something vile out too—and fast. The body knows what it knows.

Looking up again from this emotional upheaval, scanning the gentle, rolling hills, these three phrases enveloped my mind:

This life is both exquisite beauty and excruciating pain.

Expect nothing less.

Accept all.

I thought I had already known the beauty-pain logistic, but this was that lesson on an entirely different, profoundly tangible level. Even though in theory I don't expect the day-to-day things in life to always go smoothly, I sort of do on an unconscious level, if I'm being honest. When things go awry, I feel as if something is wrong with the world, as though it should not have happened. As if I was handed a contract when I was born and told, "Sign here on the dotted line. This ensures all will go well."

Let me put into greater context why this event was so timely and meaningful: I have been struggling with an ongoing heartbreak for years that has recently escalated. All the while, I've been trying to figure out how to navigate the pain that didn't seem to be getting resolved anytime soon. I was trying to reconcile how to still live a joyful life regardless.

What I gathered from Almighty God through my roadside experience was this truth: *Life carries extremes of both inexpressible splendor and downright torment. This side of heaven, expect it. It's the dark tunnel and it's the lit, brilliant circle at the end. Can you live with both? The only other choice is denial and numbing. Here's how we'll get through it: embrace the reality, embrace the juxtaposition, as you embrace Me.*

Aging and Johnny Depp

This morning, my husband stood in the doorway of our bedroom, his palms open with that potential-minefield look on his face, and said, "Now, I don't want you to take this the wrong way . . ."

Here we go.

I waited for Part 2 of that sentence. Upgrading to a white-flag-waving smile and with one palm up like a peace officer, John began again. "I don't want you to take this the wrong way, but I just want to make sure that all these ongoing online charges from places like [and here's where he began to mispronounce the names of these skin-care manufacturers, as well as I can remember] Rodent Field and Unicorn and Nuremberg are all correct. I'm seeing charges for, like . . . *a lot of money* . . . and I don't have any way to verify."

I smiled a comforting smile and said, "Nope, we're good. They're fine. I hereby officially verify. Ship-shape." Punctuating the sentence with my signature *we-can-move-on-now twinkle*, I turned back to my laptop and continued typing.

Hey, work with me here.

Recently I'd watched a TV pundit attempt to make his point about a celebrity—a woman of a certain age—who had made an outrageous statement about a well-known political figure. (Okay, it was about Donald Trump.) I agree that what she said was awful. But in the pundit's litany of derogatory terms used to lambaste this woman was the word *aging*. As in, *She must really be shameful. She's aging.*

So what, the pundit isn't? A newborn isn't? We're all aging unless we're dead.

And today? The actor Johnny Depp flippantly spoke about actors and assassinations and specifically about President Trump. After I saw the clip, I knew that someone in the media would weigh in on Johnny's comment, but I also anticipated that they would include *his aging state.* Sure enough, as I was prepping dinner with a twenty-four-hour news channel on in the background, a political commentator included the age detail, as in, *He's a has-been, used-up, burnt-out, an inconsequential nobody.* For the record, while I do think what Johnny Depp said was uncool and even dangerous, I still have to ask: what does his age have to do with it?

I hear it all the time. While listing all the distasteful, horrible, ghastly things about somebody, people will include the term *aging* as if it's a character flaw: "And not only that, they're . . . [wait for it] aging!" SHUDDER.

What up, America? Eastern cultures more highly revere the fellow humans who have flipped more calendar pages. These individuals are seen not as losing value and becoming less awesome, but as growing more awesome—superior, even. They are treated and spoken of as having attained wisdom and virtue, as being literally and perhaps spiritually closer to heaven.

Admittedly, a few years back I didn't feel so personally slighted at our society's derisive view of aging. I didn't really notice. But I've crossed over since then. Now I'm officially taking care of The Skin I'm In, and A Little Dab Will Do Me. (You may not get that "little dab" reference if you're not of a certain age. Sorry.) Still, I feel there are certain things, good and true, that I instinctively understood as a child, that I need to preserve until I'm no longer In This Skin.

So to summarize . . . *Growing up: a good thing.*

When we're little, we're asked what we want to be when we're older.

For five minutes as a child, I wanted to be a nurse. For a while I wanted to be a comedian. Sometimes as adults we pay someone a compliment by saying to them, "I wanna be you when I grow up."

As a child, I noticed my grandma Josephine's long, shimmery silver hair when she released it from its all-day bun before bed. I saw her shiny mane as quite beautiful and of great value, perhaps gaining value. Just like her.

When I grow up, I hope this will be the way I see not just my hair but my worth.

At Least It's Not

D on't cry" are the words some of us heard as children. As adults, we may even hear "Don't cry" from another adult (sometimes in not-so-many words, and sometimes in those exact words).

I believe the interpretation is, "Don't cry, because it's hard for me to see you hurt. If you stop crying, we can both be okay. We can go back to what we were doing before the tears, and get on with it." Also known as: *Pull yourself up by your bootstraps. Walk it off.*

Whether you're in a mild dilemma or have been slammed by an unthinkable, heart-wrenching, life-altering catastrophe, almost inevitably you'll hear someone say, "Well, at least it's not . . ." If your dog just got hit by a car: "At least you still have your cat." If you miscarry: "At least you still have Johnny," or "At least you can get pregnant again." If your spouse just died: "Well, you're still young; at least you can remarry."

We want so badly to make hard things go away that we shoo away the awkward moment, the painful tear—*that thing* that makes *us* uncomfortable. Unfortunately, we're also diminishing our ability to truly comfort and get in that space with the one who is hurting.

Our efforts to offer a glimmer of hope and a cup of consolation, while well-intentioned, tend to leave the sufferer feeling either a little unseen and unheard, or else absolutely certain that he or she is alone. But to minimize or deny the pain doesn't zap the pain; it only serves to isolate the sufferer.

Another way we do this is by jumping in too quickly when someone wants to apologize to us. We interrupt them—maybe even mid-apology—with what seems like a magnanimous grace-gift, essentially putting up our hand and saying, "Oh no, that's okay. No worries. You're fine." It would usually be better, though, to let the apologizer hold that space and speak the truth they have reached.

These moments of honest discomfort and pain are maybe some of the very best meeting spots—sacred places—where real heart-action happens. As awful as they can feel, they are gateways to the good stuff. Doors to true intimacy. Treasures to hold dear and near.

David of the Bible—a man after God's own heart—knew it. Knew that his heavenly Father valued his tears. His Daddy didn't try to minimize them or whisk them away; He tenderly gathered them up, permitting all and discarding none. Not . . . one . . . drop.

You keep track of all my sorrows. You have collected all my tears in a bottle. You have recorded each one in your book (Psalm 56:8 NLT).

In our humanness, we won't always know exactly how to honor someone's grief, but at least we can give them permission to grieve by not rushing past the hard moment. We don't have to come bearing words either. Usually just our presence, a hug, shedding heartfelt tears of our own, is enough to join them in their sacred place.

Don't Throw Away the Oar

I'd just hopped on my bike and was speeding up the hill toward the path near my house when I spotted an old, rusting, full-of-history-and-romance aluminum rowboat in a neighbor's driveway. I saw a sign attached at the stern (I speak *sailor*), and I hoped it said, FREE. It did. Better yet, it said FREE BOAT. Nice and specific.

Craning my neck to continue scanning as I passed it, I fought the temptation to turn around and get a closer look. I knew what John would say if I asked about us adopting it: "NO. Where are we gonna put it, Pammy?"

Regardless, I instantly began the role-play in my head and, fortunately for everybody involved, I had the perfect answer. Letting off my pedals, I pulled a quasi-U-turn, making a wide circle that landed me right in front of the boat. Coincidence? I think not.

Planting my feet on the pavement while straddling my bike, I pulled out my iPhone and snapped a photo. An old salt came out from his side yard and said, "Hello, ya interested in my rowboat?" I half-expected him to pull out a pipe and start puffing.

"I sure am. But I know what my husband will say." Then I told him what my husband would say.

My new best friend/old salt Tim and I chatted briefly about the boat; he mentioned that he'd bought it from Sears long, long ago and that he still had the receipt and outdated registration paperwork. I asked him if it was watertight, and he confirmed she was more than seaworthy. *I loved her.*

I told Tim I was going to zip on back home and talk John into it—I mean . . . ask him how he might feel about bringing her home. I knew I had to act quickly 'cause this girl was gonna go fast. (Great bargains always do.)

Since our house wasn't even a block away, I was home in a jif. With time of the essence, I rested my bike against my car in the garage, walked into the den, and employing my best community-college psychology, I squealed, "Guess what!? I found something you're going to LOVE!"

John smiled. He knew he would not love it. He knew he would not know where to put it.

I pulled out my iPhone and showed him the photo like I was showing him our new grandbaby he didn't know about. I then proceeded with the full, New-Old Rowboat Campaign.

John interrupted and said, "Pammy, where's it going to go? We have nowhere to put it."

"Oh, easy. Even if, and that's a huuuuggge IF . . . even if we don't use it as an actual, functional rowboat on the lake or whatever, I have a great idea."

He smiled. It was the gently pained smile that says, *I'm losing this battle.* I recognize that smile. Vaguely. Truth be told, I don't see it often enough.

Continuing my pitch, I said, "Remember when we were in Italy a couple weeks ago at Lake Trasimeno, and Claudia recommended that restaurant in front of the lake? Remember that rowboat right outside the entrance? It was used as a planter, and it was BEeeeauuuutiful. Just beautiful. Remember?"

In my heart, that rowboat and this rowboat felt like fate, the wonderfully divine kind.

My husband shook his head. He didn't remember the boat in Italy. So I helped him.

I described the lovely planter rowboat and presented all sorts of ideas regarding how—in the event that we don't use it for an actual boat—we could create a piece of rowboat art ("rowbart") in our yard. You see, if not function, then form. And what a neat reminder it would always be of our recent trip to Italy! This was simply a *no-risk venture*.

Doing for John what he could not do for himself, I employed second-quarter community-college psychology and put things in motion. Pulling a panther-like, quasi-U-turn in the den, I walked toward the garage door and encouraged my husband. It's what I do. "C'mon. Let's go look in the yard and do some imagineering."

Pushing against the arms of the den chair, he slowly raised himself and walked behind me toward the garage and out the side door to the back yard. He listened as I pointed to the various places where the rowbart could be showcased. Super bubbly, I suggested, "Let's hop on our bikes and go take a look. And fast. If we don't now, she could be gone."

Following me to the garage, John raised a leg and threw it over the side of his bike. Now in the saddle, he followed me up the hill. As we approached, I could see that someone was looking at Our Boat. "See? See? What'd I tell you, John? She's gonna go fast."

I introduced John to Tim, and we chatted about the boat, with Tim mentioning the weathered oars. He held the more battered of the two, showing that the blade was broken at the top—half shattered, really. It looked like a ravenous shark had taken a bite out of it. He joked that he didn't recall how it had broken; that perhaps it happened as he was beating off a big fish.

The conversation suddenly moved to marriage. I've noticed the past few years that John often tells strangers how long we've been married. He tends to do this after I make a joke, or do or say something out of the ordinary (*their* ordinary, not mine). John will pipe up with some variation of, "Can you believe it? I've been married to this woman for . . ." and then fills in the number of years. In the beginning, it made me a little self-conscious to know that people might be doing the math in their head and figuring out that if we've been married *that* long, we must not be Gen Xers.

I'd thought the reason he was offering the information was out of sheer pride, almost bragging in a sweet way. But now that I think of it, maybe it's more of a desperation cry, as in: *Please, please, help me! I've been married to THIS WOMAN for alllll these years!* (Note to self: next time John makes such a statement, check for sad tear in his eye.)

Tim casually responded that he and his wife have been married fifty-two, in a *I hear you, we're part of the same club* kind of way. I was, and I'm sure John was, genuinely impressed with Tim and his wife's record. Fifty-two years. Respect.

Since it really seemed we'd be taking Rosie home (yes, I had named her between our house and Tim's—"Rosie," as in "Row-sie," as in *Row, row, row your boat*; and Rose-ie, as in a planter full of roses), I begged off because I needed to get my bike ride in before the summer sun got all sweltery. I left John and Tim to it and started pumping up the hill.

I have some of my best reflective times on my bike rides. As I thought about the conversation with Tim, I began to see the rowboat as a marriage metaphor. Even the oars took on meaning. Especially the battered, broken one.

During my ride, I started to feel a little guilty about (1) pressuring John to adopt Rosie, and (2) leaving him literally on the asphalt with my—as John calls it—"presumed close." (He's in sales.) So I stopped pedaling and sent the following text: "If u really don't want it, it's ok. Really." And I meant it. Maybe the thing was too big and would turn into an eyesore that we'd just end up having to kick to the curb like Tim had. I didn't think so, but it could happen. I texted, "I'll make lunch when I get back."

He texted back, "It's ok. It's already in the back yard. :)"

"This is gonna be a messay," I wrote back. I didn't plan on typing that, but it eked out. And then, so did this, unexpectedly: "Don't get rid of the broken oar."

And then John: "Oar what?"

And then me: "That was beneath both of us."

Truthfully, I didn't want John to throw away the broken oar because, chances are, it can be fixed. As in any "veteran" marriage, he and I have encountered our share of sharks circling our rowboat in our thirty-three years together, and sometimes they've taken a nasty chunk out of our oars. But we've been able to beat them back. Plus, the broken oar is a good souvenir for how hard you fought off that big fish that wanted more than just one bite but didn't get it.

In any case, if a new tool is needed, you can buy one online. I checked. Still, my recommendation stands: If at all possible, don't put your full-of-history-and-romance, seaworthy rowboat on the curb. Maybe she needs to be reinvented, repurposed, rather than discarded.

As for our Rosie, I'm not sure what we'll do with the old girl. I do know I love her. If we don't put her on the water, maybe we'll plant some roses in her and watch her bloom.

Trash Day

Rounding the corner in my car at the street that intersects mine, I was shocked to come upon a gargantuan garbage truck with its big rear end sticking out into my lane. What caught my attention was not only that it was parked, but that it was parked so haphazardly. Then I saw the feet on the curbside near the truck. Two feet attached to two legs, attached to a back lying flat on the ground, face up, inches away from a soft patch of community grass.

Looking a little closer, this prone body seemed to belong to the garbage man who belonged to the truck. Was he taking a break? I sure hoped so. I wanted to think he was relaxing in the shade of the truck on this dog day of summer, but as I passed by, he didn't seem to be moving. So I too parked a little askew and jumped out, yelling, "Are you okay?"

The guy raised his head and gave an enthusiastic "Oh yes, I'm fine! Thank you!"

So he was just taking a rest after all. Maybe eating an egg-salad sandwich with a bottle of Tazo iced tea in hand.

In the moment I had yelled out to him, various thoughts rushed in: *If he's not okay, can I give him CPR? Maybe mouth-to-mouth? Would I? Yes, of course I would. I'd be super scared. But I would do it.*

I'd be scared for three reasons. One, it's been a long time since I taught preschool and was trained in performing the lifesaving technique. Two, he's a stranger. And three, he's a garbage man touching all that stinky garbage. Not with his mouth, but still . . .

I've sometimes wondered about sanitation workers: *Why would anyone want to do such a grimy job?* I've wondered what the upside might be. Can the pay really be that good? I never investigated. Not until now. Turns out a Sanitation Department job is a coveted position. (One man's trash truly is another man's treasure.) It's darn good pay with dang good benefits, especially if you're in it for the long garbage haul. Perks, pension, everything. Well, everything except the respect of *some*.

Many moons ago, when I was nurturing a would-be sarcasm career, I'd occasionally respond to "What does John do for a living?" with "Oh, he's a sanitation worker." With a poker face, I said this just to see the response. Hilarious, right? No, not really. (I've tried to grow up since then. Some days it sticks; some days, not so much.) I wasn't meaning to subtly denigrate the sanitation industry; I just liked testing people and then, of course, getting the payoff of the laugh. "Oh, Pam, good one!" is music to my ears. So, as I was asking the prostrate sidewalk-man if he was okay, I was simultaneously signing up in my head that *yes, if I need to, I'll give him mouth-to-mouth*. Not because I'm the heroic type, but really and truly because I thought of Jesus in Matthew 25:40 saying, "Whatever you do for one of the least of My brothers, you do for Me." And then of course I felt bad for classifying this man—this sanitation worker—as a "least of." I mean, what makes him "least"? I mean, week in and week out, he gets rid of my trash, and I don't even thank him. Hmmm, sounds like someone else I *do* know, the ultimate Sanitation Worker who not only got rid of my trash in one fell swoop but who keeps the neighborhood of my heart tidy, week in and week out, day in and day out.

As the old hymn says, "Jesus takes my burdens away." He also takes my trash away. Considering my elitist, snap judgments about people doing thankless jobs such as taking my stinky refuse to the dump, I'd say Jesus has His work cut out for Him with the task of handling my heart.

Let's circle back to Jesus's words "the least of these." I just took a closer look at the passage. I've always assumed Jesus meant the marginalized—the hungry, the thirsty, the homeless, naked, sick, and imprisoned. And if I'm honest, I would maybe even stretch that to mean garbage collectors. Anybody who is perceived of as "lower status." But then my mind rewinds to the actions of my parents. The parents who rescued me at eighteen months old. Who swooped in and picked me up and gave me a home when I didn't have one.

I was, quite literally, "the poor and needy." They fulfilled my long-standing interpretation of Jesus's words in Matthew 25, and I've loved them for it. The downside is that, in a very toxic way, I carried the stigma of the poor and needy. I carried that shame until the day my heavenly Father gave me a new classification as His very own.

Now I'm wondering: *Have I been reading Jesus's words wrong?* It appears I may have. Examining the context of these verses in Scripture, it's very possible that Jesus was referring to His disciples, His representatives, people who were modeling themselves after Him when He spoke of "the least of these." So if my new interpretation is on point, then my garbage man is more like Christ than me, job-wise. He's a metaphor for Jesus because he hauls my trash away.

At the end of the day, we're all the same. We all have trash. Even the trash guys have a trash guy. We're all on the same level—garbage men, CEOs, presidential nominees, butchers, bakers, sarcasm makers—all flat on our backs, all needing the Breath of Life to save our lives.

Baggage

Standing alone at Love Field's baggage claim in Dallas, awaiting my bags and my ride to our family reunion, I was reminded of my new normal. Up until recently, I had never had one piece of luggage go missing—and I've certainly done more than my share of traveling. But after having a world-class luggage mishap less than three months prior, I knew what was possible. Now when my luggage is even the slightest bit sluggish coming down the chute, I get nervous.

That world-class "mishap" I mentioned? John and I were two of the seventy-five thousand travelers affected by the British Airways global system outage on May 27, 2017, that began at London's Heathrow Airport (and also affected nearby Gatwick). Having arrived at Heathrow on a Virgin Atlantic red-eye from Los Angeles, we'd checked in for our connecting British Airways flight to Barcelona, checked our three pieces of luggage (John's one, my two), gotten our boarding passes, and headed to our gate. Not long after, the slow drip of information and misinformation, direction and misdirection, detours and debacles that made up the humongous IT "meltdown" commenced.

We'd begun hearing rumors of a computer hack while we were in the terminal. The hack had supposedly thrown a wrench into tens of thousands of travel plans, severely disrupting British Airways flight operations worldwide. (We'd later find out that the disruption was a result of human error. *Ooopsie!*) Our intended itinerary was pretty straightforward: a two-hour layover and change of planes at Heathrow, fly to Barcelona for a couple of days, and then move on to Italy.

Not so much. Among other adjustments, we ended up having to skip Barcelona altogether.

This global systems outage forced us, along with about a googolplex of people at Heathrow (and at connecting airports worldwide), to have to figure out our Plan Bs. John and I couldn't just rebook a flight on another airline to Barcelona since we were without our bags. Before we could go anywhere, we needed our three pieces of luggage. So those of us who were stranded were herded to baggage claim like cattle . . . but not before going back through passport control and customs, which we correctly imagined would be Nightmare Central. As we all inched forward in the serpentine line in Terminal 3, everyone was on their phone, trying to come up with an alternate plan.

When we finally arrived in baggage claim, the relatively controlled chaos of the herd erupted into full-scale bedlam, with twenty or so overflowing baggage carousels slowly spilling out thousands of bags, one on top of the other. People were now losing it—babies, teenagers, old people, and menopausal ladies like me were yelling, pushing, crying; some even sat on the floor begging airport personnel for help, claiming to have a "special case."

John and I worked as a tag team, scouting out the multiple carousels. I'd found John's bag; meanwhile, neither of us found my two bags. This figured.

After multiple hours of jostling for position, checking and rechecking each baggage carousel multiple times, and standing in lines for assistance, I was spent. Our search ended when multiple announcements were made to clear out of the baggage claim area NOW; there would be no more bags today other than what had already been spewed forth from the belly of the baggage beast. We were told to go home—or just go somewhere. Our bags would be shipped or delivered to us "sometime," they said. I had no doubt this meant that I would get my luggage eventually . . . but with the enormity of bags British Airways would have to sort through, it would be long after we'd returned to the States, after our European vacay. This was obvious.

My middle name isn't "Never say die" for nothing, but even I knew there was nothing more to be done there that day. Someone (me) had to accept reality. Already having given up, John (lightweight) was outside. However, there was no way I was departing London without my bags, so John and I booked a hotel and grabbed an Uber and headed to our Hyde Park hotel.

My husband and others cheerfully suggested we just "go shopping" and re-create my luggage while we were in this lovely Mayfair neighborhood, and then proceed with our two-and-a-half-week trip to Italy and Croatia. *Simple!* Except that this was a packing effort that was carefully thought out for weeks, maybe months if you factor in slaving over a hot computer, shopping online for interchangeable travel clothing right down to the cushiony socks—a process as complicated as a septal myectomy (Google's most-complicated surgery). And have I mentioned that I hate, loathe, detest "Look at the bright side!" comfort? ~~Pollyanna~~ John knows now like he's never known before.

Later that night, a barebones British Airways website finally was back online with an official statement that said, "Don't come to the airport tomorrow for your bags." So we set the alarm for 4:30 a.m. to go to the airport tomorrow for my bags.

Just after sunrise, as the Uber dumped us onto the Heathrow asphalt, I reconciled the odds. Considering the magnitude of lost luggage—and the tens of thousands of people who, just like us, were trying to retrieve their possessions—I admitted to myself how minuscule our chances were that we'd get *my* luggage, and so I stopped walking and put my hand on John's sleeve (a fresh sleeve he was able to change into *since he had his luggage*), and eked out a teary-weary, "I think we ought to say a little prayer."

Following a bit of begging to the Baggage Claim Operator in the sky, we entered the terminal and tag-teamed it again. I waited in one massive line as the worst-case-scenario default while John went hunting for A Better Way, having no idea what that might look like but willing to try since we *had* called in the Higher-ups.

I'll spare you the blow-by-blow minutiae, but what happened next can only be called a miracle. (Take it or leave it.) People sometimes talk about "divine appointments," or refer to "serendipity," but I know that The Better Way my husband found inside of an hour defies all logic. As though he was a VIP, John was literally ushered through the masses by high-level personnel and brought straight to my sweet little, meticulously packed polycarbonate luggage. Moments later, as I saw my husband approaching with my long-lost spinner suitcases gliding behind him, I knew I'd never loved him more.

My friend Tiffany has a story of delayed baggage too.

Tiffany grew up in Paxville, South Carolina, along the I-95 corridor. Paxville is a little town known for its poverty, and a little town where everybody knows everybody. Growing up, Tiffany and her heroic mom lived on welfare and food stamps. In a way, they raised each other. Tiffany's parents divorced when she was a year-and-a-half old, and from then on, she carried a daddy-wound.

Like me, Tiffany has been well acquainted with stigma and shame. She was the student in elementary school who got the free lunch; the kid to whom the Methodist Church provided Christmas. When Tiffany and her mom were finally able to move into Section 8 housing, it felt like a palace compared to the previous place, which had no indoor plumbing.

One of the primary ways Tiffany has always expressed herself is through music. I've seen her perform rhythm and blues, and that girl's got both pipes and moves. Tiffany began singing at six years old and eventually grew her God-given talent into a career. Along with singing professionally, she began working for an organization that provides shoes for impoverished children around the world. In fact, the first time she and I met in the flesh, Tiffany was delivering shoes to my IMA girls in Guatemala.

Tiffany knows that the life she now lives makes no logical sense and that, statistically, she "should be" living along the I-95 corridor to this day, maybe with several babies with different daddies.

In Tiffany's twenties, she met and married a man, had a rocky relationship, divorced five years later, was engaged to another man, broke that off, and dated some more, but no one felt quite right. She was getting used to just being alone, her hope dwindling at the reality of her life.

In early 2014, Tiffany was in the Caribbean delivering shoes to children when she found herself in conversation with a woman she had just met. As this providential chat evolved into a more intimate discussion, the woman boldly asked her, "Do you want someone in your life? Do you pray about it?" When Tiffany told her that, yes, she did want someone in her life but that she did not pray about it, the woman quoted James 4:2: "You have not because you ask not."

"Think of it this way," the lady said. "Children ask Santa for a bike for Christmas because they want one. Ask God for a 'bike.'" So Tiffany began asking God for a bike. Literally. Using this code word, she started praying, "God, I want a bike." Sometimes she'd whisper to God about her shiny new bike.

A few months later, Tiffany landed at home in Nashville after traveling for over twelve hours, and she was exhausted. She arrived at Baggage Claim 8, only to discover that United Airlines had sent her bag on another plane coming from Houston, where she had connected earlier in the day. She couldn't go home and come back to retrieve her bag later because her car and house keys were in her luggage, so she decided to sit down on the floor, accept what was, and make good use of her time. She came up with a to-do list and then pulled out her cellphone and called a man she'd been dating—something she'd been putting off. Tiffany knew she only wanted to be friends, and she didn't want to waste his time.

After the call, she realized she'd closed another door in her hopes of meeting someone to spend her life with, but she had no doubt it was the right decision. She was feeling a certain peace with her life in general—she loved her job, she loved singing, she was healthy and reasonably happy . . . Sitting there on the floor, she said to herself, *Okay, God; it's just You and me.*

God had another idea, however. And that *idea* was about to walk by.

No sooner did Tiffany say those words than the most beautiful man she'd ever seen approached Baggage Claim 8. As she watched him, she thought, *Why can't I date a guy like that?* Then she noticed something: it appeared that he was looking *at her*! Just to verify, she glanced over her shoulder to see what might be behind her that had caught his attention. *Nada.* When she realized he was eyeing her as much as she was eyeing him, Tiffany got up, walked his way, and happened to see a friend. Saying hello and making small talk, the friend providentially asked, "Are you dating someone? Please tell me you're not still single!"

Tiffany, fully aware that this beautiful man was within earshot, answered her friend with something along the lines of "Well darlin', now that you mention it . . . no, I ain't!" in her Southern twang. Moments later, the friend's bag circled around on the conveyor belt and she was on her way. Most Beautiful Man inched toward Tiffany. She saw his initials, LJT, on the backpack behind his megawatt smile.

Lo and behold, Tiffany's delayed baggage and Most Beautiful Man's bag emerged from the chute, one on top of the other. Most Beautiful Man (and now Chivalrous One) helped schlep Tiffany's bag off the conveyor. Tiffany responded by asking, "Do I know you? Where do you go to church?" (I told you, girl's got moves.) He said his name was Lee, he answered where he attended church, and he added that he was also a musician, which for Tiffany was a major NO, but *ah, that smile*. Right when she was feeling brave enough to give him her business card, he asked if she'd like to have coffee. Lee texted her that night, and the rest, as they say, is *his-and-herstory*.

When Lee walked into their first date at Nashville's Bongo Java, Tiffany noticed his nice gams, which she calls #legsteaks. Apparently Lee was an avid bicyclist. (God is so clever. She had been praying for a bike, remember?)

As time went on, Tiffany and Lee got to know each other on a deeper level and revealed some of their respective baggage. Like me and every person on the planet, they both had some. Lee told Tiffany that he was freshly divorced and in recovery from alcoholism.

Two years later they officially joined forces, becoming "TiffanLee" in their romantic, twinkly lit backyard. One of the many things she's impressed with is that her welfare is Lee's priority. She'd never had that from a man. Especially from her own father. Eventually, Tiffany found closure about her dad, recognizing that he too had baggage from his childhood—baggage he just couldn't put down—that impaired his ability to love her well and handle her little-girl heart in the tender way she deserved. That is when she was able to forgive his mishandling and all the loss she'd endured because of it.

Tiffany says that one of the reasons she's living a happily-ever-after story—biking off into the sunset with Lee—is because she went so long without someone like him. This has made her appreciate, all the more, the miracle she has now.

As I'm standing here at Love Field baggage claim recalling Heathrow's pandemonium, I see my spinner case emerging a little late, but here. And I'm thankful. Thankful not just for luggage that arrives as it should, but thankful that it's possible to leave baggage shame, walk into love field, and risk our hearts to handlers who we are confident have our best welfare in mind.

Tiffany and I can both attest: it's the only way to fly.

Cream of the Crop

I remember how skeptical I was when my siblings and I talked about going in together to buy our dad a computer for Christmas one year. I don't know if I said it out loud, but I definitely remember thinking, *He'll never use it.* Not only did I think Dad's fingers were too stubby to hit one key at a time, but *It's too complicated for him. Soooo NOT agricultural.* But wouldn't you know? Not only did he use the computer, the man's on Facebook today.

Ninety-nine percent of the photos of my dad in his current Facebook collection are there because I tagged him in them. Some are shots I've personally taken—such as the one of him from a few years ago, wielding a sledgehammer in our terraced garden like a man half his age, knocking posts into the deep earth to support the tomato plants. Another one I snapped on the sly, after all his work was done in the garden that day. He's on his back in a wet T-shirt and shorts, floating on a raft in our pool, bronzed from the sun except for his ivory-white legs. Resting on his face is a pair of black Jackie O sunglasses, fake rhinestones in the corners glistening in the sun. He told me he'd found the glasses on the side of the road awhile back and liked them.

Many of the black-and-white photos I've tagged Dad in are ones I snagged and scanned from his and Mom's treasure trove at their home in Northern California. Even as a little girl, I was drawn to the cardboard box in the closet at the end of the hallway, the box I could escape to and hide inside. Every now and then, I'd plant myself on the floor there, unpack the bounty of family history, and spend hours poring through images of my most favorite underdogs and tenacious lovers.

One photo features my dad displaying his harvest: a purple cluster of grapes that came from his own vineyard. The photo looks to be from the late 1960s or early 1970s. The bevy is so massive it stretches from the tips of his fingers to the top of his disproportionately beefy forearm. He looks proud. And thankful. Maybe lucky.

My dad wasn't a farmer until he became a farmer. As he'll tell you, he didn't know how to grow stuff; he just did it. Like most things he got involved with, he had no formal training. He just decided it's what he wanted to do, and he hit the ground running, never looking back.

He may give his shoulders a little shrug and say that he's been "lucky," but I can translate Dad's definition of that word. Sure, he paid his dues and worked hard—harder than anyone I've ever seen—but to him, *lucky* mostly means *blessed*. He's had a few key people come alongside and give him some pointers at different times, but he probably finished the task before they were done showing him how to do it. He is the quintessential self-starter and little pipsqueak that could. His true grit drove him to finish what he started if he saw value in the seed of an idea.

When my dad was in the army stationed in Korea, he didn't smoke, and what he *did* drink was minimal, he says. He will admit one vice, however: he liked to play cards and shoot dice. With his signature shrug and smirk, he also says he "won all the time." He allowed himself only twelve dollars a month to play with, and he would faithfully send the rest of his paycheck to the bank in Warren, Ohio.

When he played, his cap was 150 dollars. Every time his winnings reached 150 dollars, he would quit and send that nice little chunk of change home too. By the time he was discharged three years later, my dad had five thousand dollars saved up. He says it was unheard of for an average Joe like him to have that much money in the bank in the 1940s. He had more liquidity than his own dad.

He came back to the States, bought a nice car, married my mom, and told his uncle Tony that he had close to five thousand dollars and wanted to buy an old house. He'd seen that he could get a pretty decent two-story home for that amount, but his uncle suggested that he could build his own, brand-new house for the same amount instead. When Dad told his uncle that he didn't know how to build, Tony said he'd help. Uncle Tony found twin 100 x 300 square-foot lots with a selling price of nine hundred dollars for the pair. My dad, spotting a promising seed, said he'd take 'em.

While working ten hours a day at Van Huffel Tube Corporation—a steel mill in Warren—my dad, with help from Uncle Tony, built his first house on one of those side-by-side lots within three months. Dad used up all his money in building the first house, so Uncle Tony offered to put the lumber and supplies needed for the second (investment) house on his own credit. "You can get a loan and pay me back," he told my dad. Dad ended up owing $7,200 and had a $40.50 per month payment.

Six months after my parents moved in, a man knocked on their door and offered fifteen thousand dollars to buy the home they were living in. Dad said, "I'll take it," and moved himself and Mom into a rental while he finished building house number two next door—which took thirty days while he continued to work ten-hour days at the mill. Mom painted the interior of house number two, and she and Dad moved into their new home upon its completion.

My dad will be eighty-eight years old next month. After watching three-plus hours of video I'd recorded of him over the past couple of years, it occurs to me now that the man just might be brilliant. His phenomenal ability to recall detail even now is astounding. Names of people, places, dates, numbers—the man is a walking, talking history book or search engine, which he also knows something about (along with Facebook).

Let's back up.

It was summertime when my dad and his buddy Richard apparently had their fill of Ohio and ran away from home and hitchhiked to New York City. With empty pockets and only the clothes on their sixteen-year-old backs, they landed where the action is, at 42nd and Broadway, Times Square. The YMCA wouldn't take them in, so they slept tucked in behind some concrete stoops for a week and were sustained by a few meals, courtesy of the kindness of strangers. Richard and my dad each landed jobs bussing tables in a high-class restaurant where they made good tips. They were permitted to eat there, but because they took advantage and ate too many free meals, they were both fired.

Next, Dad got a job in Brooklyn at a chrome-plating factory where, he says with that signature eye-twinkle and smirk, "You had to be fast." He was making seventy cents per hour for the first couple of weeks, but then he was called into the office and given a five-cent raise. His coworkers were incensed because most of them had been there for years, and now here's this young pipsqueak, already getting a raise. So half of them quit. After four or five months, Dad decided it was time to move on too, and so he headed home to Ohio and returned to high school. But he quit for the last time after a month and decided to join the army. His uncle Ray tried to talk him out of it—even tried to bribe him by offering to buy him a car—but Dad said, "No thanks." He knew a car wasn't what would take him where he needed to go. It wasn't a promising seed.

Since he was only seventeen, Dad required parental consent to join the army, and my grandpa signed the paperwork. At the recruitment office, Dad was told he'd have to wait two weeks before he could be sent to boot camp in Fort Jackson, South Carolina, because it would take that long to get his bus ticket. Dad didn't want to wait two weeks, so he said he'd buy his own way. Two weeks into boot camp, he and his fellow recruits found out they'd be shipped out to Korea.

Starting out as a driver in the motor pool, Dad was fast-tracked to his main job as head mechanic. Even though he'd had absolutely no training in this field, his superiors saw what he could do after he devoured the information in four mechanical books. Spotting a seed, they gave him authority over the entire motor pool. He was in charge of 150 vehicles—jeeps, fire engines, ambulances, road graders, bulldozers, two-ton trucks. Even the sergeants had to come to him to check out a vehicle, and Dad could deny anyone. He says he would routinely drive over to the mess hall with either "his" fire engine or ambulance, always sounding the siren to announce his arrival. "Ciarolla's comin'!" his buddies would say.

In the service, Dad was routinely put in charge of things that were unfamiliar to him and given authority over others because of his ingenuity, tenacity, and work ethic. He was even placed as the lead soldier in marching formation despite being the shortest man. I don't know how it's done these days, but Dad says that back then, it was the six-footers at the lead. He was so *so* not the norm. And yet, in every role he's had—as a soldier, a mechanic, a steel-mill worker, a mason and bricklayer, a farmer, a construction-company owner—he blew through the ranks by the sheer force of his spirit, his creativity, chutzpah, and willingness to sweat. Time and time again, he stunned his superiors by his gumption, and very often he became the boss. He was consistently the cream that rose to the top.

One of my favorite roles he chose to play was that of father to me: my pop, the cream of the crop. When he had an opportunity to become my dad, he said he'd take it. From what I've been told, he didn't give it a second thought. Maybe he saw a promising seed. Feeling my own shoulders shrug, I guess we were both a little lucky . . . and a lot blessed.

Little Seed into Big Tree

Jesus told His disciples a story about a farmer who goes out to plant his field. Some of the seed falls on a hard path and is snatched up by birds or trampled underfoot by the people who walk the path. Some of the seed falls on rocky soil where it does germinate, but since there's no depth to the dirt, the roots get no water and the sun burns away any growth. Some seed falls on soil littered with weeds, yet the weeds choke the seedlings before they can bear any fruit. Finally, Jesus described the seed that is planted in good soil. It produces healthy seedlings and grows into a full crop, blessing the farmer with beautiful, sweet fruit.

Both literally and figuratively, all life grows from a seed.

My friend Jeni, partnering with the giving organization Soles4Souls, brought her troop of fifteen teenagers (a service group formerly known as Roots and Shoots—the Napa Valley chapter of Jane Goodall's global youth organization) to the IMA school in Guatemala. Their team arrived by bus with a load of shoes in tow, ready to play with and serve our 150 IMA students. This was the first time I'd met Jeni in the flesh, and our hearts instantly connected.

Jeni is a big, big tree. Towering. If I could, I would add this description to her current Facebook page, where she describes herself as a mom, social activist, nature girl, graphic designer, and wearer of heart on sleeve. All I know is, I've never seen anyone more committed to volunteerism and helping others, be it in her Napa, California, backyard or Haiti, Honduras, Peru, or Guatemala.

I've heard her say that her passion is to ease others' suffering. Whether she's bringing aid to the poor or homeless, helping victims of a local fire, mentoring teens, or conducting shoe, clothing, or diaper drives, Jeni's always brainstorming (heartstorming) with a sky's-the-limit mind-set, coming up with new ways to give back while exposing her teens to a lifestyle of service. In other words, she's planting seeds.

Last year, Jeni received the Community Champion Award, which recognized her passion for humanitarian work. But accolades are not why she does what she does. Jeni gives back because she's received. A seed was planted in her.

The seed of Jeni's volunteerism began, in part, because of her parents' strong example. But this seed also grew out of a painful time in her own adolescence, which is one of the reasons she grew her work with teens into her own nonprofit called Teens Connect.

Connecting is what Jeni does best.

When she was thirteen years old, Jeni, who felt she didn't fit in, began fantasizing about suicide. Thinking about it gave her a sense of relief—it was the only way she could envision to end her pain and loneliness. Soon she began using drugs and alcohol. By the time she was fifteen, Jeni was in rehab, where she was forced to feel her pain. More desperate than ever to end her life, she wound up in a psychiatric hospital, which only served to make her feel even more isolated.

Jeni didn't trust anyone, including the therapists who promised that life would get better if she followed their program. But halfway through her hospital stay, she met a therapist named Rob. Rob had long hair, tattoos, and rode a Harley. Rob was rough around the edges, just like Jeni. He didn't say a lot, but for some reason, just being in Rob's authentic presence calmed Jeni.

"He was real," she says. "Once, after I had promised him I would stop hurting myself, I cut my wrists and was placed in solitary confinement. He stormed into my room the next day and said, 'You promised me you wouldn't do this! I believed you! I'm not going to waste my time if you're not going to stand by your word!'

"It was the most real thing anyone had said to me during that period," she recalls. "In that moment, I knew I wanted to get better. Because somebody—this one person—really saw me and heard me and cared about me when everyone else was too afraid to listen. Rob saved my life."

She has since learned this: "We want those struggling to have the courage to ask for help, but what is equally as important for the rest of us is having the courage to listen. As a parent, the hardest thing we might hear is that our child is in so much pain that he or she wants to die. As a friend or family member, we might not know what to say if someone we love is in that kind of pain. It might be easier to ignore these cries for help, especially because we don't know how to help. But just acknowledging someone's pain can make all the difference. We don't need to have answers."

We can hold space, as Rob did for her.

Rob's authentic presence not only saved Jeni's life; it planted a seed in her heart to reach into someone else's life and try to ease their suffering. And that seed has turned into a harvest.

Sometimes it has started with putting new kicks on a little girl's feet. Jacque, one of Jeni's teens from Napa on the bus that day in Guatemala, connected with Veronica, one of my little IMA girls, and Veronica felt really seen and heard. For Jacque, a seed took root in that budding friendship.

After having spent the day shodding little feetsies, playing soccer, doing art projects, and enjoying a pizza-and-soda party with the IMA girls, Jeni's group gathered together for their meeting with her. Jacque told Jeni that she'd had an epiphany that day; that she was so inspired by the experience and her connection with little Veronica that she had changed her mind about what she wanted to do after high school. She knew her career path—and even more importantly, her *life*—would be geared toward easing others' suffering.

A Greek proverb comes to mind: "A society grows when old men plant trees whose shade they know they shall never sit in."

Because of Jeni . . . because of Rob . . . because of Jeni's parents . . . Jacque became a seedling that day at the IMA school. It's not hard to imagine Jacque growing into a towering tree for having sat under the shade of Jeni's tree.

I've heard Jeni use some terms that have stuck with me. She talks about hearts being "broken open." It makes me think of that heart-soil Jesus talked about. When someone clears space to listen and see us in the presence of our suffering, it can do wonders in our hearts. They may become fertile places for the falling seeds to take root. And when seeds take root, they have opportunity to grow into large trees that cast a wide circle of shade for others.

To care nothing about notoriety this side of heaven, wanting only to ease another's burden in their hard, rocky place so as to provide a comforting patch of shade—this is the essence of true service, the field of harvest in a suffering world. This humblest of places is where I see Jeni standing tall.

Pony Rides

I just started reading Anne Lamott's new book, *Hallelujah Anyway*, and as often happens when I read Anne, her insights fly off the page and into my heart. Sometimes they make a stop at my throat first, and give it a nice little grab. This time the line was, "Fair is where the pony rides are."

Yes, *that. That's* where "fair" is. Fair is at the fair, and only there. Must. Not. Forget.

I am stunned by how often it slips my mind that life never promised to be fair. I do remember the pony ride though.

I was on it. Once. For me, that one live pony ride at the county fair sufficed. I was good-to-go for a lifetime. From then on, I stuck to straddling my Pammy-size toy rocking horse at home, or my broom-style horse that I could take on the road, or occasionally, the coin-operated pony ride outside of Kmart.

I couldn't have been much more than five years old that day at the fair. It was your classic pony-ride-in-the-round where the real-life ponies walk the same circular path while hitched to a mechanical "walker." The walker is like a wheel on its side, with the spokes connecting the baby horsies on the ends and the hub-cap engine in the center.

This is a pretty controlled environment, considering that the ponies are not only tethered to the contraption but there are also carnie attendants walking alongside the riders, providing human reinforcement and maybe emotional encouragement. There's not really much room for error. Yet somehow, some way, before my fellow riders and I had made even a couple of revolutions, my pony bucked and I went flying. At least that's how I remember it. (I guess it's possible that my little five-year-old fanny just slipped off the mini saddle and slowly slid down onto the dirt path in a semi-soft landing. But I'm going with the more exciting version.)

Whoever said that when you fall off a horse you have to get right back on probably wasn't ejected from a budding bronco at age five at the fair. When you think about it, that pony ride wasn't all that fair to me. Note to self: revisit Anne's fair-is-where-the-pony-rides-are theory.

My pony tale aside, this idea of life and its unfairness is a big sticking point for a lot of people, and has been for a long, long, long time. You could fill entire libraries with the number of accounts that have been written on the subject, fiction and nonfiction alike. One of the most interesting treatises on the subject is the Bible's book of Job. If you want to talk about unfair, pull up a few of ol' Job's "and the hits just keep comin'" experiences. If you read to the end of his story, you see that God made right what Satan made wrong, but God kind of got in Job's face with the "Who do you think you are?" line of questioning—certainly a little more than I personally would have voted for, considering that God deemed Job a full-on, righteous dude.

In my lifetime, I've heard personal stories of good people who undergo one life-shattering tragedy after another. Scripture says that rain falls on both the righteous and the unrighteous. A lovely young woman gets married and is excited to settle down, only to struggle terribly in her marriage, which ends in divorce. She finds love again, remarries a wonderful man, and before they can have children and make a family of their own, she is diagnosed with cancer and dies a torturous death. Others survive an illness, only to receive an unrelated diagnosis later and endure an altogether different battle. Or they lose a precious child to an illness or accident, or some random act of violence is wreaked on their family, or they have a financial catastrophe and go bankrupt. The possibilities are endless.

We tend to think that if you have one big trauma, drama, illness, or tragedy in your lifetime, you should have met your quota. But it doesn't always work that way. Not to be a drag, but sometimes it's one thing after another and then you die.

Sorry.

The Bible's book of Proverbs is filled with wisdom ("You reap what you sow," etc.), but its general truths are not absolute guarantees. Sometimes life takes twists and burns in a scorching way that makes no sense at all. My friend Terri knows about this.

Terri and Brad's first baby, Kara, was born one month premature. The couple's trip to the hospital that day included all things they hadn't imagined—Kara's four-pound, seven-ounce birth weight, her emergency heart surgery, and hours upon hours of testing. Her eventual diagnosis was severe cerebral palsy, and because of her heart anomalies, doctors said her prognosis for survival was five years.

Thirty-three years later, Kara has not only shown the doctors a thing or two, she's shown all of us who have been lucky enough to meet her a thing or two—or maybe a hundred thousand things or more. And all of them have to do with tenacious love.

Because Kara's anomalies were nongenetic, Brad and Terri planned for a second child, and four years later, they were excited to have a baby sister to bond with Kara. But once again, their lives were turned inside out by a medical diagnosis. Tayler was born with malrotation of the intestines, and half of her intestines had died in utero.

At seven days old, Tayler came down with a lethal infection caused by the high-risk bowel surgery she'd undergone, and Brad and Terri were told that their baby daughter was dying. Before the surgeon and attending nurses untethered Tayler's oxygen supply, her morphine drip, and the IV fluids that were keeping the newborn alive, a visiting pastor rose from his seat and suggested that those surrounding the incubator join in prayer. When it came time for Terri's turn in the circle, she prayed, "Jesus, Your will be done."

Tayler's stay at Choc Hospital was six months long. Today, at twenty-nine years of age, Tayler is a beautiful ballroom-dance instructor. Tayler also has shown the doctors (and all of us) a hundred thousand things or more.

Less than two years later, Brad and Terri had yet another precious daughter, Paige. Paige was born with no health issues and has been a champion for her sisters. Today, Paige is a crime-scene investigator, a wife, and a new mom. I can vouch that Papa Brad and Nana Terri are completely insane-in-love with their luscious grandson, Lucius.

In the early days of Kara's two-month hospital stay, Terri struggled with the unfairness of life. She begged God to heal her daughter. His answer was not a no; His answer was, "A healing is coming." Terri believed this, but what she didn't know then was that the healing would be for herself. Today, Terri is healed of her need for Kara to be healed or to be anything other than who she is. Terri lives *God's will be done.*

Terri's life verse is Jeremiah 29:11: "'For I know the plans I have for you,' declares the LORD, 'plans to prosper you and not to harm you, plans to give you hope and a future'" (NIV). Through her daughters, Terri has learned some of life's most challenging lessons about not only fairness but surrender and enduring hope. If Kara could speak, I can only imagine the hundred thousand ways she would vouch for her mom and dad's constant, exhaustive, utterly unconditional love. Her sisters have plenty of such stories themselves.

The expression "Pay it forward" didn't start with the 2000 film bearing the phrase. The general idea—that a recipient of a good deed ought to repay it to another instead of the original giver of the kindness—has been documented at least as far back as the ancient Greek play *Dyskolos*, but I believe Lily Hardy Hammon coined the actual phrase in her 1916 work *In the Garden of Delight* when she wrote, "You don't pay love back; you pay it forward."[12]

Terri and her husband, Brad, have paid love back by paying it forward over and over again. Rather than give in to a tempting bitterness at life's inequities, they have chosen to respond by giving back. In her

---

12 Lily Hardy Hammond, *In the Garden of Delight* (New York: Thomas Y. Crowell, 1916), 209.

book *Simple Acts of Kindness,* Terri not only provides a painfully honest glimpse into their experience of raising their three daughters, but she offers creative ideas about how to help someone whose heart is broken over the unfairness of life.[13] What had been given to her and her family during some of their darkest times inspired her to establish Simple Acts Ministries, a nonprofit that encourages anonymous giving. Hers is an example of facing earth's unfairness honestly and victoriously, where a person chooses to say "Hallelujah" anyway.

Life doesn't always match up with our plans. Sometimes we get violently bucked; sometimes we slip down onto the dirt slo-mo style. Thomas Watson said, "When God lays men on their backs, then they look up to heaven."[14]

No one gets off easily. Not even ponies. Not even at the fair.

I know people who, based on life's inequities, have decided against believing in the existence of God, or if they toy with the possibility of a God, they conclude He can't be good. In their rationale, they choose against God to somehow punish Him. But in the apostle Paul's second letter to the Corinthians, he puts things into perspective, reminding us that this life isn't "it" (which I personally find to be key). As often as I forget that life isn't supposed to be fair, I also forget that this life is not the be all, end all; it's not the Big Lebowski, the whole shebang, the entire enchilada, the main event. Paul tells us, *Hey, by the way, what's happening down here and now? It's teeny, relative, and temporary. Focus on the big picture, guys*:

> *Therefore we do not lose heart. Though outwardly we are wasting away, yet inwardly we are being renewed day by day. For our light and momentary troubles are achieving for us an eternal*

---

13 Terri Green, *Simple Acts of Kindness: Practical Ways to Help People in Need* (Grand Rapids, MI: Fleming H. Revell, 2004).

14 Thomas Watson, *A Divine Cordial: Romans 8:28* (Lafayette, IN: Sovereign Grace Publishers, 2001), 42.

glory that far outweighs them all. So we fix our eyes not on what is seen, but on what is unseen, since what is seen is temporary, but what is unseen is eternal (2 Corinthians 4:16–18 NIV).

It's pretty much impossible to convey an ethereal experience. You have to have built a whole lot of credibility in order for someone to suspend earthly rationale and completely buy in to a claim. And even then, it's tricky. I get it. I've heard stories from people about their religious or spiritual experience, and my typical response is just to listen. Whether I believe it or not, I'm not about to tell someone they didn't experience what they said they experienced. Truth is, I don't know.

A few years ago, I had a dream while on vacation in Cabo San Lucas that continues to inform the way I do my life on most days. The dream had two messages: First, that all my worry here on earth is pointless because God is not only carefully paying attention, He's paying my pain and worry forward to a greater good, a higher purpose within a bigger, unseen, unimaginable master plan. The other message was: *This world is puny. Don't get caught up here, because the world on the other side is mind-blowing, heart-bursting beauty too exquisite to even begin to fathom with your earthly mind. So, please, just trust. You'll thank Me later.*

The combined physical, emotional, intellectual, and spiritual "feeling" I experienced during that dream and in the moments after awakening sustains me today in some of my most difficult, flat-on-my-back, "unfair" moments. With this perspective, I am reminded to look up to heaven and choose to say "Hallelujah" anyway.

Spaghetti Western

After my full-blooded Italian parents moved our family three hundred miles north from the big metropolis of Los Angeles to a teeny town in the San Joaquin Valley, they quickly got to work building a home and a new life for us. Our home included a thirty-acre vineyard in the backyard; a couple dozen chickens that produced legit, farm-fresh eggs; a substantial, thriving garden; fruit trees; and three little pigs.

That was all going so well that my dad decided it was time to expand his farming repertoire and invest in cattle. Disgusted by the quality of meat he'd seen in the stores, he decided he wanted to raise a few calves of his own and feed his family beef he knew would be top quality, healthy, and nutritious. Nothing but the best ground beef for my mom's homemade meatballs and spaghetti. So he set out in his truck and trailer one day and headed to the local livestock auction house in Riverbank, a town perched above the Stanislaus River—and a short drive southwest from our house.

The calves at the auction were deemed "wild" (Dad was told they weren't accustomed to being in the city or around city folk) and had only recently been brought down from the mountains. They were so wild, in fact, it took four men to get Dad's one new calf, which we'll call "Angus" from here on out, into the trailer.

Keeping watch in his rearview mirror as he drove carefully through town, Dad saw Angus growing agitated, thrashing about, and kicking like, well, a wild animal. The calf was fighting so hard that he broke free from his head restraint, and then, before my dad could do anything about that, Angus gave another swift kick. The trailer gate flew up and open, and Angus bolted out into traffic. In the center of an intersection.

My dad slammed on his breaks, grabbed his lasso from the seat beside him, and began running after the fleeing bovine. Angus's first stop was the local bar. He literally ran in one door and out the other with my dad trailing behind. (I can only imagine the patrons doing a doubletake and concluding they'd had one too many.) On a full-blown tear, Angus proceeded to patronize other businesses and homes, destroying property and fences right and left. Kids were screaming, adults were hollering, and soon my dad had about twenty or more frantic followers—his posse—running after him as he ran after his rogue cow all through town and back around again.

At one point, a young woman—unsure how best to help—yelled out to my dad, asking if he'd maybe like a glass of water. My dad yelled back, "No, but can you call this number and tell my wife to get someone over here to help me!?"

My mom later reported that the woman who called her said, "There's a little fat man running through town chasing a cow!" She knew right away it was Dad. My mom phoned a couple of neighbor boys, and they agreed to drive on over to Riverbank. Not knowing exactly where to go, they figured they'd just look for the crazy cow parade.

Hours later, my dad, exhausted from running in frenetic circles, watched Angus do something he didn't anticipate: the cow suddenly stopped and calmly lay down on the asphalt near his original escape point.

My dad stopped too, walked over to his pickup truck—still in the intersection with the door wide open and keys in the ignition—and drove it the few yards over to Angus.

Dad opened the gate on the back of the trailer.

Angus looked at my dad, stood up, walked over to the trailer, and stepped inside.

My dad closed the trailer, secured it as best he could, and everyone went home.

Angus met his match, outlasted by the fastest little fat man in the West.

Storm Trooper in Blue Mascara

I won't lie. I have very limited understanding of what a storm trooper is. I did go to one Star Wars movie about a hundred years ago for a family outing when the kids were little, but I fell asleep midway through. I know there were some underdogs in it. I think. I deserve mom props, as it was an opening-night, midnight showing. I was trying to be a trooper and not a party pooper.

Though I'm still a little sketchy on storm troopers, I believe I have a pretty good handle on what a trooper is. At least my definition, anyway. The way I define a *trooper* is someone who is an underdog with tenacity and a bent toward ragamuffinry. One thing for sure—a trooper is a little love that could or who would. All of my siblings (all nine of us ragamuffins abandoned by our biological parents) meet this criterion, and our most recent family reunion in Texas was further evidence.

As I have at each of our family reunions, I play the role of *wacky baby sister* and provide the comic relief. On the last night of this latest reunion, when my brother-in-law/reunion cohost Steve told me that a tornado had touched down nearby and that we'd need to get into the storm shelter (what I mistakenly called a *bomb shelter*), I didn't believe him. I laughed it off as a pathetic attempt at payback. Did he know with whom he was dealing? I thought not.

It wasn't until he put his smartphone in my face with the "Take shelter immediately" weather-service warning that I was a believer. Moments later, the shrill emergency sirens (serving as a nice exclamation point, I might add) also backed up Steve's claim.

After having a cozy hour or so in the storm shelter with all my she-sibs, a brother-in-law, one visiting grandma-neighbor, and her three precious grandchildren, we emerged none the worse for the wear and maybe a tick more bonded having weathered this storm. Our matriarch, Barbara, offered up a couple of prayers and suggested we sing hymns to keep our esprit de corp intact. This seemed to work nicely, as no one freaked out. Our shyest sister, Patty, even belted out a solo.

To my knowledge, this tornado had done no damage, but we did get to see some exciting, driving rain before and after the storm-shelter stay (and through the teeny windows during), not to mention a spectacular thunder-and-lightning show afterward. The humidity was about 4,000 percent. Also, I have about eighty-five mosquito-bite souvenirs.

If I had my own storm shelter like my sister Barbara and her husband do, I would paint a name on the side of it like a ship and I'd call her *Shelter in the Storm*. I might even crack a bottle of the bubbly over the side of the old girl, so strong and capable, holding all of us sisters snugly together and offering such nice acoustics for a sing-along. I posted pictures on Facebook, and people commented on how relaxed and happy we looked.

How could we be smiling during a tornado? It's what we do.

I think it's perfect that *trooper* rhymes with *swooper*, a term I have singlehandedly originated. A *swooper* is, as I've mentioned already in this book, someone who swoops in to help others. All my siblings are good swooper troopers. Give-backers. Not a bad one in the bunch. They have fostered babies and older children; they serve their communities; they are active in their churches; they volunteer in different capacities; they bring art into the world; they all help in one form or another; they all beautify and put love out into our universe. My sister Beth provides a pro bono preschool for young ragamuffins who need a little extra something before kindergarten. The school incurs all costs for materials and doesn't charge a penny.

Each of us has our different takes on what happened to us as children—the whys, hows, and what-fors—but no one, not one sibling, is bitter for the storms. Speaking for myself, while I have smiled a lot, I've also cried a good bit too.

The nine of us have been exposed to life's elements and often given shelters in the storm. We're survivors, in part because we've been a shelter for each other. I have some precious, primal memories of my older siblings providing an empathy that no one else could quite understand or offer.

On one of the relatively seldom but always painful occasions I spent with our biological mother, I became panicked as though I was suffocating, and I ran out of her presence. Weighed down underneath an unbearable shame, I literally ran into the arms of my sister Ruth—my littlest big sister—and simply with the look in her knowing, chestnut eyes beneath her long blue eyelash curtains (I'm guessing Maybelline's Great Last Royal Blue Mascara), she waved me in and became a sanctuary in my storm. I don't think I was old enough to wear mascara at that time, but I wanted the beauty my big sister had. She swooped in, met me where I was, and gave me refuge and protection in her strong, storm-trooper arms.

I found this trooper easy to define—hers was a little love that could, would, and still does. And I am safe.

Soar

This week we celebrate my mother-in-law's birthday. Since I'm a woman of a certain age, I know it's not nice to mention *the birthday age of a woman of a certain age.* Not unless she volunteers it herself. Let's just say, Sandy has spent some time hovering here on this great planet, and leave it at that.

Yesterday was the official family get-together at an indoor skydiving place. I was the self-appointed official photographer due to a shoulder injury that prevented me from putting on a flight suit and catching air like everyone else. Poor, rich me. So I grabbed my new iPhone 7 with its 12-megapixel camera, and a front-and-center spot, and I snapped 345 photos of my family having fun taking flight. All the lights and bright colors and unabashed exhilaration made my job sublime—which, by the way, Webster defines as "supreme or outstanding."

Another definition of the word *sublime* is "raised up, high up."

While our family was waiting our turn, we got to watch other fliers in the room's vertical, zero-gravity wind tunnel. In between paying fliers, the professionals would put on brief acrobatic shows to demonstrate what was really possible if you knew what you were doing. It was a pretty jaw-dropping exhibition, defying the laws of physics and what our eyes typically behold on a Saturday afternoon anywhere outside the doors of iFly Ontario (California).

While we waited, I noticed a simple sign on the wall. For a few bucks more, you could upgrade your flight to "high." Most of the people I'd watched only went about head high, if that, but a couple of the fliers soared high to the top. Perhaps they were the ones who'd paid a little extra, along with being a little more adept at following directions and handling their bodies. There was a handful of fliers unable to lift off at all, even waist high. I wasn't sure why they struggled so much, but I felt disappointed for them. Maybe their bodies were too rigid, or they weren't tipping up their chins enough. I silently hoped this would not be the case for Sandy. I mean, *what a disappointing birthday celebration that would be for her.*

A moment later, I overheard Sandy say through a smile as she watched other fliers, "I want to go high." The way she said it made me think of how my voice probably sounded as a little girl at the park when my dad would push me on the swing: "Higher, HIGHER! I want to go HIGHER!"

When it came time for the birthday girl's turn, she not only did not struggle *at all*, but she got right up from the get-go. As if she'd done it a thousand times. (Maybe she had, in one way or another.) She hit the ground flying, embodying Webster's definition: she became "raised up, high up." She went all the way to the top in that vertical cylinder, as if she'd been shot out of a cannon. I craned my neck from my position on the floor and watched her shoot vertically, reaching the pinnacle. I tracked her wildly exuberant smile the entire time, like a "Look, Mom, no hands!" little child.

She did everything right. She kept her chin up and her eyes toward the ceiling (and perhaps beyond). She knew what was *really possible.* In her way, she knew what she was doing.

Personally, I've had a sublime time watching her fly since I was a child. I've never seen her take her eyes off of heaven. At iFly Ontario, and in all her days hovering over this great planet thus far, this high-flying birthday girl is *supreme*; she is *outstanding.*

It's a joy watching her fly.

#TooBlessedtobeStressed

Along with the hashtag on social-media posts, I see the line "Too blessed to be stressed" on T-shirts, and every time I do, I want to hurl red paint on the person wearing it and scream, "Too blessed to be stressed?! You're in denial, people!"

Now, before you start throwing fresh produce at me in protest, let me acknowledge upfront that not everyone who wears the shirt or posts the hashtag is in denial. *I know this* intellectually! But my initial, immediate reaction is always a visceral one, as unfair as it may be.

Blame it on the movies in part. I saw the film *Stepford Wives* as a young teen, and it resonated with me as the-robotic-way-I-do-not-want-to-be-perceived-in-life. Katherine Ross's character was so creepy she made me cringe. In a less creepy way, but with the same sugary-sweet fakery, was the film *Pollyanna*. Hayley Mills played a little girl who, like me, was an orphan, but with nauseating, over-the-top optimism.

Considering that strain of stress comes as a result of "adverse or very demanding circumstances," the T-shirt wearers and hash-taggers always make me wonder: Have they never felt the press of demanding circumstances? Are they such spiritual gangstas that they don't ever feel a little beaten up? Ever? Are they so rock-solid that they don't ever get a little wobbly?

On my grumpier days, I think, *Lies. Lies. All of them, lies.* I simply don't believe there's a soul dead or alive, regardless of station or religion or hard-drive wiring, who is so coated in Teflon that they don't sometimes feel a little burnt, a little crusty, a little stuck. What's more, as a Christian, I have a question for the Christian hash-taggers and T-shirt wearers: Why do we want to perpetuate a Photoshopped Christianity? Who does it serve?

Jesus Himself stated that in this life, His followers will have trouble. He also reminds us that we ought to take heart: we can have peace because He has overcome the world (see John 16:33). I take this to mean that there *will* be stress (trouble) while we walk this planet, but if we link arms with Christ, who is the great Overcomer, we will also overcome—in the meantime and particularly in the end. Does that mean we must message a perpetual state of unragamuffiny, bleached-smile, blemish-free bliss? I don't think so.

As a rule, I tend to overthink and complicate things. (You're really not surprised at this, are you?) It's the thorn in my side, my number-one means of self-sabotage. In theory, *Oh, how I love the idea of simplification!* But in reality, to simplify too much is sometimes a disservice to ourselves or others.

When we abbreviate to create some of our slogans, for example, we're trying to cut out the fat. We want to travel light—fit things into a carry-on—so we remove some extra socks. But later in our trip, our toes get cold. Or in the case of "Too blessed to be stressed," we risk stepping on a lot of toes that have already been crushed by hardship and adversity.

Admittedly, we are—and always have been—diverse people with diverse experiences. Not everyone has endured the gut-wrenching turmoil of Job. We all know people who are more innately joyful and upbeat. They sort of float a little higher, seemingly impervious to pessimism. Maybe it's because they've learned to be grateful regardless of their circumstances. (If that's you, would you mind giving me a few pointers?) Or maybe they've never known tragedy, and so they just don't understand how bad it can be when one is struggling through addiction, trauma, or mental illness. That's why, if I had my way, no one would wear the shirt. It implies that a person is weak if they're too stressed, and not only weak, but *not blessed*.

Kahlil Gibran's sage writing about joy and sorrow in *The Prophet* both haunts and comforts me:

> *The deeper that sorrow carves into your being, the more joy you can contain.*
> *Is not the cup that holds your wine the very cup that was burned in the potter's oven?*
> *And is not the lute that soothes your spirit, the very wood that was hollowed with knives?*[15]

I've said that I emerged from the womb with a saltshaker in one hand and a ripe tomato in the other. I also was born with a thirst for authenticity. I've truly always *wanted* the truth, even if it was painful. Lies seem pointless to me, a waste of everyone's time.

It hasn't only been truthful *input* I want either; *output* is necessary for me as well. Rather than stick my head in the sand, I've literally stuck my hand into Bocca della Verità—the mouth of truth—in Rome. I'm a truth teller.

But wait! Hold on! (Insert *screeching tires* sound effect.) It occurs to me *at this very moment* that, even as a person who theoretically has always valued authenticity, I placed that truth against my heart for a long while, folded my arms over it protectively, and hugged it to myself, *not* presenting it to the world. I didn't think it was something others would be willing to see.

In venting about the hashtagging T-shirt wearers in this essay, I forgot that, in a way, I wore the shirt for a long time too, until I was ready to risk showing the less-desirable truth I'd written on my own heart and

---

15 Kahlil Gibran, *The Prophet* (New York: Alfred A. Knopf, 1923), xx.

hidden under the self-serving self-hug. It's for this very reason that I recognize the behavior in others: *You spot it, you got it.* Or, at the very least, *You had it, so don't forget it.*

I heard author Carol Kent say in an interview: "People don't identify with our successes nearly as well as they identify with our sorrows." As a little girl watching *Pollyanna* and *The Stepford Wives,* what repelled me is what I ended up embracing. I was guilty of showing the world only what I thought the world should see about me.

We tend to mistakenly think that they will like us better if we're *too blessed to be stressed.* Yet we're all ragamuffins at one time or another, which means we need a new slogan. How about this one? *When we're real, we heal.* #TrueThat

Risk vs. Reward

I'm no mathematical genius or financial whiz by any stretch, so I don't understand much about numbers or investments, but I do get the concept of risk versus reward.

I've been a grateful member of a twelve-step group for over ten years. In the beginning, I shared in the group occasionally. I did it often enough to avoid getting out of the habit, knowing that, once I felt I didn't need to be transparent, I'd opt out on the regular. Eventually, though, I got lazy and stopped sharing altogether. And before I knew it, a few weeks of silence became several months—and then several months became . . . far, far longer.

As a rule rather than an exception, I took and didn't give back. For years. But a couple of months ago, I admitted what I've known all along: there is no substitute for the reward of (appropriate) risk.

For example, when I go to group and silently sit through a meeting, I'm sticking my baby toe in. So it's only my baby toe that gets wet. When I actually share out loud, I dive in and am immersed. And I come out dripping wet. I also walk out of the group having had an entirely different experience. It's not because I said anything profound. It's because I invested, and there's always a return there. I did the opposite of what I wanted to do. I risked. I got out on the dance floor and shook my metaphorical groove thing rather than hanging back and being a wallflower.

Entirely. Different. Experience.

I find that the same principle applies with the concept of "Let go and let God." To me, it's very risky to admit that some things are completely outside my control and there's really not one stinking thing I can do to produce a different outcome. Yet if we intend to live by faith, we must not only admit it but live it.

We're commonly told, "Trust your gut. Trust your instincts." But I beg to differ. I beg to differ because Jesus said it's an upside-down world. "Don't trust your gut," He warned. "Instead, do the opposite." It's what's twelve-step groups call "contrary action."

Our gut doesn't always hold the right instinct. Sometimes, when I rely on what Scripture calls *my own understanding*—trying to manage a problem, improve it, or defeat it without any help from above—I get in the way of what God might want to do. To put up my hands and say, "You do it, God; I'm letting go," tends to be the riskiest of ventures. The consequences can seem too much: If I let go 100 percent and do NOTHING, what if nothing gets fixed? If I give up 100 percent control to another Power and *crazily* imagine that Power as having all power and authority in the universe, what will be the reward? Will there even be a reward? Is there a guarantee in advance?

Nope. It's risk.

Though what's at risk, *really*? Jim Elliot, one of five missionaries who was killed while attempting to bring the news of Jesus to the Huaorani people of Ecuador in 1956, stated, "He is no fool who gives what he cannot keep to gain what he cannot lose." In a recent twelve-step group, someone said something that was maybe equally as brilliant—and beautifully, ridiculously simple. This guy said, in effect, "When I really, truly accept that I am powerless over something, and I relinquish the false notion that it was a job for me to do in the first place, I am somehow, ironically, freed, empowered."

In those group meetings, we hear the wisdom of *not* doing the same thing over and over again in hopes of a different result. Our default—our gut—leans toward the supposedly "safe," familiar choice we've made in the past (which, incidentally, hasn't worked). But in the radical, upside-down, inside-out, upturned world of Jesus, where we are "all in" and making the uncertain choice, that is often where the reward has the best payout. Where the ultimate dream gets realized. Where the miracle can actually begin.

In 2012, my friend and brother-in-law, Warren, passed away of a brain aneurysm at fifty-one years of age. I have many sweet memories of him, and one comes to mind that illustrates this opposite way of thinking. The details are a little fuzzy, but I remember the basic concept.

Warren was telling me about a child (it may have been one of his own sons) who had left a bike out overnight. The next morning, the boy was relieved that the bike hadn't been stolen. Rather than reprimand the youngster for leaving the bike out, Warren told him, "It would have been fine had it been stolen, because the potential thief probably would have really needed it."

I listened while shaking my head internally. I thought it was an irresponsible position to take, especially for a dad who's instructing a child. My quick judgment lasted only a moment, however, before I thought of Jesus's words when He said, *If anyone wants to take your shirt, give him your jacket as well. If someone slaps you, turn the cheek and say, "Hey, what about this side? Give it a whack." If someone forces you to go a mile, say, "How 'bout we double that?"* (See Luke 6:27–30 for the actual version.)

When Jesus was on the earth, He stood on a hillside and taught that His kingdom would be a don't-trust-your-gut realm. A radical, contrary-action world. A do-good-to-those-who-hate-you place. A give-away-what-you-have-to-gain-true-wealth territory (see Matthew 5:1–12). This language not only challenges our long-held value systems, it is completely foreign to our natural sensibilities.

I struggle with this illogical logic. Is there possibly some sort of balance we need to strike? Doesn't Jesus want us to be good stewards of our resources? Protect what He has provided? It sounds so risky, metaphorically or otherwise: *Does Jesus really want us to leave our bike outside for someone who might need it?*

It's my instinct that I ought to end this with an answer. Perhaps the real answer is the question.

Come as You Are

I'm not proud of it, but I'm not a model citizen. Some folks are eager to discharge their civic duty, but me? Throughout my adult life, every time I've been summoned for jury duty, I've managed to figure out an excuse—and my excuses have always worked.

The fact that I don't want to serve is ironic because courtroom dramas are one of my favorite movie genres. (For the record, the others are psychological thrillers, prison dramas, stories on the high seas, and anything that makes me both howl and bawl.) Yet for whatever reason, my image of jury duty has resembled my experience of traffic school: me with a just-kill-me-now face, sitting hour after hour in a stiff folding chair as monotone voices drone on and I watch my ankles morph into thick, iron chains, all the while thinking about my leftover gnocchi in the fridge at home.

When I received my last jury summons, I thought, *The jig is probably up. Maybe it's time.* That was part personal responsibility talking, and part awareness that the courts nowadays seem to be on to people like me, having made it more difficult for attorneys to discharge potential jurists at the drop of a cockadoodie excuse. I discovered this after reaching the part on the summons where it says, "To request a postponement, excuse, disqualification, or exemption from jury service, please visit www.blahblahblah. blah." That's when I realized I'd better be a big girl and do the right thing. So I went to www.blahblahblah.blah, scanned the information about things like dress code, and requested a postponement for a new call-in date, which I was granted. This would not be a get-out-of-jail-free card; it was a kick-the-can-down-the-road card. Nevertheless, this was growth for me.

It should be noted here that I somehow failed to enter my new call-in date on my calendar. Thus, jury duty completely slipped my mind until one summer morning, while I was still groggy and still prone, I remembered. My eyes slammed open cartoon-style, and I popped up and began rifling through my papers in my "filing system." When I found the court information, I saw that my check-in date had been a few days prior, and by the looks of it, it was very possible I'd have to show up *this very morning* at the courthouse. I logged on with my group number and, sure enough, I was supposed to be in Newport Beach—which was 15.8 miles away—in twenty minutes. In no traffic it would take half an hour, but the morning rush "hour" could double the time.

I ran to the bathroom for a quick glance in the mirror: *Uh-oh.* Matted, four-day-unshampooed hair, ponytail askew, a keen sense of unbrushed teeth, and mismatched PJs (what I call "Pammy's jammies" or "Pajammies," which generally are torn or threadbare *anything*, as long as they're soft and comfy). Translation: I was in my full ragamuffin uniform.

My mind flashed back to what John had said: he'd answered the jury-duty call several times before, and every time he's physically reported in, he's one of the masses who quickly gets dismissed at the first station, the orientation room. "No biggie, honey," he'd told me. "You just sign in, sit in a chair for a quick hour or so, and they dismiss everyone except a handful; and odds are DEFINITELY in your favor that you'll be headed home in no time."

He'd said this with such confidence. So, with my husband's assurance, trust in my heart, and not much choice, I threw on my Rainbow sandals and pushed the leather to the metal, heading to court in all my Pajammies glory. *How humorous it would be to get a speeding ticket on the way to court*, I thought. HI-LARE-E-OUS.

Well, John's odds were a little off. I made the first cut and was sent with a whittled-down group of fully dressed, probably God-fearing, respectable people to seats in the back of a courtroom that looked to be straight out of a movie scene. Next step: our group would be cut to twelve (plus a couple of alternates).

Eleven people were called, and I began to breathe a sigh of relief.

Next thing I knew, I was dubbed Juror Number Twelve.

Sporting unbrushed hair and teeth, a faded, tattered tee, men's boxers covered in baggy sweats, and with flip-flops on my flippers, I flopped over to my seat of honor, audibly hearing the *flip-flop-flip*. When my number was called, I stood for my initial interview before the judge, the lawyers, my fellow civil servants—an entire courtroom of nicely dressed people—to ensure I was up for the task. I don't know about you, but when a dude in a flowing black robe is seated at an elevated, polished desk in front of the great seal of the State of California, I give 'em the straight scoop sans any *blah-blah-blah* excuses.

Moses knew about *blah-blah-blah*. When God wanted him for duty, he came up with several juicy "I don't think I can" excuses: *I'm really not up to it . . . I don't know much . . . No one will believe me or listen . . . I don't know how to talk well . . . Not me—send anybody but me.* Now, I admit that when I think of Moses and the burning bush, or Moses confronting Pharaoh, I sometimes see a virile Charlton Heston. (I won't lie.) But when I look at Scripture, its truth surpasses the impressive theatrics of Cecil B. DeMille's epic 1956 production.

Fully aware that His chosen people were suffering horribly as slaves, God tapped Moses to step up as their leader and human deliverer. Moses wasn't so confident. He was like, "Say what? You want me to do what?" Moses pulled out all the excuses. God made His case, citing examples such as Abraham, Isaac, and Jacob—all flawed men who suffered serious lapses of faith and judgment at different times, but whom He mightily used. God assured His appointee, "If I can use them, Moses, I can use you. And Moses, I will be with you. I will equip you. And by the way, it's not about you!"

In 1983, my friend Tina—a stay-at-home wife and mom of a two- and a five-year-old—received a divine "summons" at a missionary conference held in Virginia. There she met Rachel Arthur and heard her desperate plea for help. Rachel and her family were Christians living in a predominantly Muslim culture in Nigeria, and mothers and babies were routinely dying in childbirth in her village due to horrible health-care practices such as cutting umbilical cords with rusty knives. Tina's compassion drove her to ask God what she could do to help. She was blindsided by his bold answer: God wanted her to build a birthing clinic in that remote Nigerian jungle. *Say what, God?*

Tina would tell you herself: She outright *whined*. She claimed she was ill-equipped—"I don't think I can. I have little kids at home. I'm just a stay-at-home mom. A simple homemaker" (silly terms, if you ask me). She had no medical training or business expertise; her limited college classes were in the arts . . . *How could You want me for this task, God?*

Tina thought she might "compromise" (my version of jury-duty postponement)—maybe take some Lamaze training, travel once or twice to Nigeria to help instruct the women on what not to do. But God wanted more. Tina soon knew her perceived "disqualifications" were precisely the qualifications God had zeroed in on. It wasn't about her; it was about Him. Not about what she could do; it was about what He could do in and through her.

Tina, along with two other "simple homemakers," Shari and Mary-Ann, got busy and established the nonprofit organization IMA (International Medical Assistance), which means "Love" in the Ibibio or Efik (African) language. *Perfect.* With their heads and hearts together, they built that birthing clinic in the jungle, and it soon became a twenty-six-acre medical compound, full-service hospital, and medical school, with a farm and orphanage to boot.

It is astounding what God can do with ill-equipped, excuse-making people.

Next, God wanted IMA to set down roots in India, and so it did, in 1989, via a mobile medical unit serving the remote areas where neither health-care facilities nor churches existed. Less than ten years after that missionary conference in Virginia, Tina, Shari, and MaryAnn heard the call to Guatemala, and that it was time for IMA to switch gears from medical service to education. They went on to open a school for girls that, as you've read, still operates today.

I was present in the early eighties when cynics forced Tina to defend her life-sustaining efforts on behalf of children who were knowingly being born into poverty. Tina tearfully stated that it wasn't about saving lives so much as it was about saving souls.

I was an eyewitness then, and I remain an eyewitness. I've seen thousands of little girls pass through the IMA doors and into the opportunity for a better life despite a harsh culture that says little girls are unworthy . . . little girls are less-than . . . little girls can't.

When I think of the examples I've seen firsthand of perceived inadequacy that morphed into the knowledge of what a powerful God can do, Tina stands out. The way this woman answered the call and gave her all has left an indelible impression on me.

As a forgetful, stinky-breathed, excuse-giving, disheveled, groggy, ragamuffin juror, I found that week of civic duty to be one of the more surprisingly interesting and fulfilling things I've done, and I'd be eager to do it again. I came as I was. I sat. I served.

Often an excuse includes a "What if?"—like Moses's *What if they don't listen?* or *What if I fail?* "What ifs" aren't all bad. Service is a come-as-you-are party, but you are not left the way you came. God suits us up, equips, and comes alongside. Meanwhile, "What if?" turns into "What if a little love could?" that goes on to say, *I think I can, I think I can, because He can.*

Come-to-Jesus Moment

Like all serious researchers, when I need answers, I consult *Urban Dictionary*. Here's how it defines a "come-to-Jesus moment":

- An epiphany in which one realizes the truth of a matter.
- A sudden, intuitive perception or insight into the reality or essential meaning of something.
- Coming clean and admitting failures.
- Realizing the true weight or impact of a negative situation or fact.
- Acknowledgment that one must get back to core values.
- Moment of realization.
- An "aha" moment.
- A moment of decision.
- A moment of truth.
- A critical moment.
- A moment of reassessment of priorities.
- A turning point.
- A life-changing moment.

A *come-to-Jesus* experience can also be called a watershed, a tipping point, a Eureka, or a Damascus Road moment.

All of these terms reflect an internal or external event that evokes a dramatic change of course—maybe one never before imagined or thought possible. Sometimes people have a *come-to-Jesus* in a time of desperation: when they are in literal or figurative prison; when they are in a foxhole, hiding and fighting; when their faces are wet with tears as they sit beside a hospital bed, their hands cradling their heavy head. Sometimes, when a person has exhausted every other avenue and they are out of steam, out of hope, and out of ideas about what else they can possibly do, they suddenly see that they've been blind for far too long.

Bartimaeus was a man who had a literal come-to-Jesus experience. He was a blind man sitting by the road, panhandling. This had become his life. Like many, he'd heard of Jesus and the miraculous ruckus He'd been causing in Jericho, and so when he heard Jesus passing by, he "saw" his chance. He yelled out, "Jesus, Son of David, have mercy on me!" ("Son of David" was a reference to Jesus's heritage and acknowledgment that He was indeed the Messiah.) Bartimaeus believed. He believed he could ask, and he believed Jesus could heal.

This blind beggar was quickly shushed by the others around him, but he paid them no mind. As he cried out even louder, "Son of David, have mercy on me!" Jesus stopped, turned His ear, and called the man forth. Jesus asked Bartimaeus what he wanted. Bartimaeus asked to have his sight restored. Jesus healed his sight on the spot, telling the man it was all because of his faith. And Bartimaeus followed Jesus.

There was another blind man. This one had been blind since birth, and he is not called by name in Scripture. We know him simply as "the man born blind," and this is one of my favorite Bible stories. I identify with this no-name man.

He'd never seen a jagged mountain range or an iridescent shimmer on a lake, but now he could see it all thanks to Jesus. The Pharisees later question the one who had been healed: "Do you know who Jesus is—is He a sinner? a prophet?" . . . and he delivers the line that always makes me gulp hard: "Who he is, I cannot say; but one thing I do know: once

I was blind and now I see" (John 9:25, paraphrase see John 9:1–25 for the context).

This humble statement resonates with me unlike any other. When I think of how I lived my life up until my late twenties, I was blind to the truth of Whose I was and how beloved I was by Him. I was blinded by insecurity, by the shame of my biological heritage, by my ragamuffin status. I didn't like my name. I'd rather have had no name than my family-of-origin name. I felt like a throwaway.

I didn't know what I didn't know.

There is so much I *still* don't know—but like Bartimaeus, now I see.

I have so much to learn. I grapple with hard questions all the time. I'm not a theologian or an apologist; I don't have a hundred Scriptures memorized; yet because of what I've seen and heard in my life, I have enough proof beyond a reasonable doubt to make the small(ish) leap of faith to cry out to Jesus. I have enough evidence in a loving God to believe He passes by, and enough good sense to come to Jesus and accept His healing touch.

From what I can tell, a humbled willingness is part of the equation—a willingness on our part to act or move. To call out. To come to. To come to Jesus.

Underdoggedness

As a timid little ragamuffin of a girl, I was a fan of the cartoon *Underdog*, the humble and lovable K-9 poet/superhero who saves many a day, sometimes making a bit of a mess along the way. He's the cartoon character who proclaimed, "There's no need to fear—Underdog is here!" each week from 1964 to 1973. I watched every episode over and over again, loving the way the sweet hound donned his cape, exhibited *a little love that could*, and shattered everyone's expectations, saving the world.

People are often blindsided by an underdog. They don't expect much. But when a lowly longshot shows his true, superhero colors, jaws drop.

I've pursued a voice-over career. I even have a VO booth in my home. So naturally, I was curious about the distinctive voice behind the cartoon Underdog of my childhood. As I embarked on a fascinating YouTube trail through old Hollywood, I learned some things about Wally Cox, the diminutive, bespectacled actor-comedian who lent his pipes for Underdog and Shoeshine Boy (Underdog's Clark Kent to Superman).

Interestingly, Wally Cox was not only a contemporary of the strapping Marlon Brando, but he was his dear friend. Some called them an odd couple, not unlike Felix and Oscar. Online, you can find friendly black-and-white still photos and footage of Wally with Brando and other mega-stars such as Dean Martin. There are even cozy images of bookish-looking Wally with buxom, iconic beauty Marilyn Monroe, who is leaning into him in the back seat of a limo on Marilyn's thirty-sixth birthday in 1962. If it's possible to see a truth in a candid photo, I would say—based on Marilyn's intent looks and laughter—that Wally was much more than met the eye.

One of the YouTube trails led me to a full episode of *The Dick Cavett Show*. Cavett was a precursor to other talk-show hosts such as Johnny, Jay, and now Jimmy. Midway through this 1971 episode, a subjectively more-handsome entertainer joined Mr. Cavett, Wally, and the British writer Anthony Burgess, who smoked a stogie and remained silent after More Handsome Entertainer took a seat onstage.

More Handsome Entertainer came out with guns and puns blazing, many of them directed at Wally. While some of it seemed playful, other comments contained quite a bite. Early on in the exchange, More Handsome Entertainer took on the Goliath persona to Wally's David. Maybe he considered Wally easy prey; a no-brainer, smackdown target to demonstrate how big More Handsome Entertainer was. That's the thing about show-offs, though: their strut only lasts a little while, until the underdog aims his slingshot and tags the cocky giant in a vulnerable place.

There was an ongoing tit for tat, with Wally gently firing off zingers of his own. Eventually, More Handsome Entertainer lost steam. Near the end, when More Handsome Entertainer was telling a story about having quit high school, Wally interrupted and said, "I think the past tense of quit is 'quat,' isn't it?"

This was the moment I fell in love with Wally Cox. This was when I understood precisely why Marilyn Monroe snuggled up to this unassuming little longshot. The audience broke out in laughter, sealing Wally's retort as his competitor's much-deserved comeuppance. In the end, More Handsome Entertainer looked like an impotent bully, as if a striped-shirt referee were holding Wally's wrist above his bespectacled, thin-mustached face—the face of a little underdog who just wouldn't quat.

Underdoggery: May the Fourth Be with You

There are a few theories floating around the Web about the origin of the term *underdog*. Most say it originated in the late nineteenth century and references a dogfight. At the end of the fight, the dog left on top (the "top dog") was the winner, and the dog under (the "underdog") was the loser. Some say it originated with the ship-building industry long, long ago, when flat pieces of timber were called "dogs." The dogs were laid over a pit while one builder (the "overdog") sawed the planks from above, and another (the "underdog") sawed from below, catching sawdust in his eyes and hair.

Clearly, in either case, being the underdog was not the coveted position. Historically speaking, the underdog has been painted as the less fortunate one, the loser. But it seems the image has evolved over time. The vibe, for me at least, is that being the underdog is now viewed as more of a virtuous station. Seen less as someone who's inferior or weak and more as a person with hidden strength or value. A dark horse, a hero who comes out of the woodwork, maybe even conquering all.

Their stories are everywhere: sports movies, TV headlines, even the Bible. Yep, it's chock-full of underdog stories. There are the classics—David versus Goliath, Moses versus Pharaoh, Job versus his whole world crashing and burning. One of my faves is the story of Shadrach, Meshach, and Abednego (see Daniel 3).

My first exposure to it may have been via a Sunday-school flannel board. I imagine myself sitting on a circular rug, legs folded, wide-eyed and wowed by the sheer theatrics, the courage these young men displayed, and the concluding twist, which always makes for a great story whether it's 600 BC or today. I don't know if I was especially drawn to their experience because I thought maybe Abednego was a nice Italian boy and I've always loved all things Italian, or because I've had a longstanding fear of fire. Nevertheless . . .

Some people might make the case that these young Jews were not true underdogs since they'd been given an elevated position in the Babylonian kingdom. But this was *after* being brought over as captives from Jerusalem, the capital city of the Jews, which the Babylonians had plundered and ruined. Young men like Shadrach, Meshach, and Abednego were recruited to serve in the royal palace of Babylon simply because of their "shine": they had good looks, brains, and brawn—the whole package. They were trophies, the best and the brightest among the Hebrews, which in turn made Babylon's king look a little shinier. Sure, they were being systematically stripped of their identity, even being assigned these Babylonian names that did not glorify their God the way their Hebrew names (Hananiah, Mishael, and Azariah) had. Still, the trio earned a reputation for an uncompromising commitment to their God, Jehovah.

Gathered together with a crowd of elites at the dedication ceremony for a golden, eight-story-high image of King Nebuchadnezzar, they were told along with everyone else, "When you hear the sound of the horn, flute, zither, lyre, harp, pipes and all kinds of music, fall to your knees and worship the golden statue. Anyone who does not worship shall be thrown in the fireplace and be toast."

The music blasted and everyone fell to their knees. Everyone except Shadrach, Meshach, and Abednego.

As jealousy is a thing now, jealousy was a thing then. Enviers and haters took notice and proceeded to rat out the rebels to the king. The king called for them and confronted them: "Is it true? You know, this is a 'you must or else' situation here, boys." The three young men didn't budge. They only confirmed, "Yes, it is true. We cannot—we will not—bow down before your statue. Do your worst. We believe our God can come through, but even in the off chance that He doesn't, we will still not worship your idol."

King Nebuchadnezzar was steamed, and so he ordered the furnace to be cranked up seven times hotter. Fully clothed and fully flammable, the renegades were bound and tied and brought to the blazing kiln's entrance by the burliest soldiers. As the burly hurlers hurled the young men into the voracious flames, the heat was so intense that *they* combusted like a wooden platter of bacon.

As for Shadrach, Meshach, and Abednego, when the king checked the furnace, his eyes widened in disbelief. "Hold on!" he said to his servants. "Didn't we throw three men into the fire?!" The yes-men agreed. Flabbergasted, Nebuchadnezzar continued, "Look! I see four men unbound, walking around freely in the fire, completely unharmed! And the fourth man [an angel of the Lord] looks like the son of the gods!" He then went to the door and called to the firebrands, "Shadrach, Meshach, and Abednego, servants of the highest God, come out!"

The king and his minions gathered around the boys to examine them—and there was not one scorch mark, not one hair singed. They didn't even smell like smoke.

King Nebuchadnezzar was so convinced by their complete imperviousness to the roaring fire that he uttered praises to the God of Shadrach, Meshach, and Abednego and decreed that no one dare bad-talk the boys or the One who had delivered them.

Not only were Shadrach, Meshach, and Abednego not fired that day, but they were given a promotion.

Whether these underdog stories come to us on Sunday-morning flannel boards, Dolby IMAX screens at the megaplex, or headlines taken from our news, their accounts inspire us to root for the disadvantaged, help us see the little guy in us all, and can give us the faith to face the fires of life . . . if we let them.

May the Fourth be with you.

Tenacious Love

Even though I felt all sorts of stigma about growing up as a foster child, I did like the attention when the social worker came to visit. I no longer remember the woman's name or face, but her visits were the one upside to being "foster." I felt kind of special. She was nice to me. We'd sit at the kitchen table and she'd ask me questions about myself—how I was, what was I was up to. She wanted to know if I was a happy little girl.

In my photo archives is a black-and-white shot of my friend Suzanne and me at church camp, and my stance is revealing. I'm standing a little awkwardly next to Suzanne, my arms at my side, not quite striking a pose (and completely unaware of the ever-flattering, hand-on-hip position). Suzanne and I both look to be about six years old. I'm wearing white canvas Ked-style sneakers, white bobby socks, white shorts, white cat-eye sunglasses slightly askew, and a white nametag on my sleeveless, collared white shirt.

I had never noticed what was written on the nametag until yesterday. The print is faint since the photo was taken at a distance, and the hand-writing appears a little smudged, but I zoomed in on the picture and realized it said "Pammy Ciarolla" (my foster parents' surname). I was born with the "Cole" label slapped on my chest, so I answered to either name. But "Cole" wasn't the name I savored. "Ciarolla" was the one I wore proudly. Looking at that long-ago photo, maybe I'm even strutting a little in my monochromatic couture.

My daughter, Cassie, is in social work. She serves as a child-and-family therapist for a community mental-health agency and works in the elementary-school setting. She's told me that she went into social work in part because of my background. I'm proud of that. I'm proud of her.

Cassie recently told me a story about a little boy with whom she works. Let's call him CLC (Cassie's Little Client). He and his family were sometimes homeless, and he spent the first six years of life witnessing ongoing drug abuse and experiencing lots of abuse and neglect. Along with his own personal nightmare, CLC witnessed the ongoing, severe physical abuse and medical neglect of another child in his parents' care—an unofficial foster child and CLC's three-year-old "little buddy." The abuse and neglect were so horrific that his little buddy died. CLC remembers checking the boy's pulse and finding none.

His parents are serving, and will continue to serve, a several-decade prison sentence for the death of the tiny boy entrusted to them. Since the parents' conviction, CLC and his two younger siblings have been in loving foster care with one family that hopes to adopt all three children. Meanwhile, the incarcerated biological father has selfishly pulled out all the stops to slow the process.

With each scheduled court proceeding, Cassie has been subpoenaed to offer her expert testimony. But because of the biological father's numerous delays, she hasn't had opportunity to take the stand until a couple of weeks ago. On that day in court, the judge decided to terminate the father's rights, though he will likely appeal the decision.

The next time Cassie met with CLC, he and his schoolmates were playing baseball. When CLC came up to bat, he connected solidly with the ball, and it soared. CLC, who hadn't yet been informed of the court's decision, threw his arms up and yelled, "Another homerun for [legal name]!" Then CLC stopped short and corrected himself: "I mean, another homerun for [future name of adoptive foster parents]!"

The Bible says, "Hope deferred makes the heart sick, but a longing fulfilled is a tree of life" (Proverbs 13:12 NIV). CLC believes in a done deal even before it's a done deal. He's made a leap of faith, hard evidence to the contrary. He's choosing to focus on the other solid evidence, that of dogged, determined love.

The appeals process could take another year and a half or more, which means even longer before CLC and his siblings can be adopted by their foster parents. Yet despite every horrible thing CLC has witnessed and personally endured, his heart is not yet sick; it still embraces hope. Apparently, his little big heart is filled with dogged, tenacious love too. Because of the tenacious lovers in his life—such as his future adoptive family and his social worker—he may even see himself as a happy little boy, strutting up to bat, solidly connecting, and then watching the ball soar for the trees of life, where his longing will be fulfilled.

On This Day

I took a stroll down social-media memory lane this morning, clicking "On this day" in the left margin of my Facebook page. Here I see my posts on this date through the years since I established my personal Facebook profile. One that I just came upon was of my family foursome—John and the kids—in color-coordinated outfits. Our son and daughter were teens at that point, but somehow they didn't complain (much) about my strong-arming.

I love this photo. Everyone was so happy, so natural. So tan. The words I'd written in the description field were: "A while ago, but one of my faves. Back in the days of forced color coordination." The actual photo was probably taken in 2003, but this post was dated July 14, 2012.

There were a few "likes," but the comments are what I noticed this morning. One was from my friend Stacie, who has since passed. Stacie wrote, "LOVE forced color coordination. Still embrace it in my mind even though no one will embrace it as willingly anymore—boo."

Stacie still shows up in my life: in Facebook reminders like this, in old texts on my phone and my Mac and my iPad that I refuse to delete. She's still listed as a contact on my devices, still one of my Facebook friends, and so on. She shows up in my mind and heart as well, even apart from these digital reminders.

I've written about Stacie over the years because she made a tremendous imprint on me and I refuse to let her memory go. It's not that I can't "move on" and do life without her; it's that her imprint stays. It just does. And I'm glad. I hope that, after I'm gone from this earth, people will smile at least a teeny bit whenever they get a reminder of me, the way I do when memories of Stacie enter my thoughts. She brought me so much happiness in her short stay on earth. I can't think of one moment when she didn't emit love. Okay, there was that one time she made a crack about how overloaded my Chinet plate was at a party, but I've pretty much let that go.

I'll never let go of Stacie.

"On this day" was also an important phrase in my wedding vows more than thirty-three years ago: "On this day I thee wed." On that momentous day in a little church in Northern California, before God and a room full of witnesses whom John and I loved, I told God I'd live my life differently from that point forward. I'd live as a partner. A partner who, not long after, would start orchestrating annual, color-coordinated Christmas photos with the children we'd parent and love together.

I recently turned fifty-five years old. (Yes, I just said that out loud.) I can't say the number doesn't freak me out a little. When you're young, a year takes f-o-r-e-v-e-r. Nowadays, I put a drop of Visine in my eyes and, by the time I'm done blinking, the year has passed. I can't believe how long it's been since this photo of our foursome was taken, and yet it seems like it was only last year.

So, fifty-five. Because time screams by now, and because I'm such a numbers whiz, I did the math the other day. It hit me that in five years, I will be sixty years old. S-i-x-t-y. In a five-year block of time, li'l Orphan Pammy will be sixty. Hopefully my life will be far from over. Nevertheless, my life-window is starting to not "close" per se, but to "get real." The question entered my mind: *What do you want to do with that block of time, Pam? What personal goals do you want to see happen in those five years? How do you want to spend that time?*

I've heard of people who, every once in a while, turn off of auto-pilot for a minute to evaluate their life goals and consider, *Which direction do I really want to go?* I haven't really done that; as a rule, I sort of take things as they come. But on this day I think I just may start to calendar some time in which to set a few official goals.

Yesterday at my Toastmasters meeting, a quote was shared that widened the eyes of my heart: "We're going to live like we're telling the best story in the whole world. Are you ready?" (Rachel Weisz in *The Brothers Bloom*).

Before she was diagnosed with brain cancer, it was probably unimaginable to my friend Stacie that she would have to leave her beautiful, tanned, color-coordinated family so soon. But once she learned her window might be closing, rather than rage against God, she sort of said, "Boo," as in, *I don't like this—not one bit, God—but I'm going to trust You and Your plan, and willingly embrace You.*

On this day I want to be intentional, making this one count. With that block of five years before me, and with Stacie as my reminder, I want to tell the best story of my fully embraced life.

For the Love of Pizza

It was John's and my thirty-third wedding anniversary trip—our fifth adventure to Italy—and what I'd officially titled on my Facebook photo album as "You and Me at Thirty-Three." We'd been down this pizza-road before too, making our way through gritty Naples to get to L'Antica Pizzeria da Michele for their famoso pie . . . but it had always been on foot from the train station three blocks away, just a hop, a skip, and a plie. This time we were in a car, driving up the Amalfi coast from picturesque Positano, and John was at the wheel.

I'd ridden shotgun in some pretty absurd traffic locales, but Naples— *ah, Naples*—really took the cake. That day, I knew I needed to keep my head down and my mouth shut tight. Meanwhile, I silently recited Proverbs 14:1, "The wise woman builds her house, but with her own hands the foolish one tears hers down," and 25:24, "Better to live on a corner of the roof than share a house with a quarrelsome wife" (NIV). I was hoping one of those would help me keep the ol' pie-hole out of commission as John "elbowed" our way on four wheels through the imbroglio. I also kept my head down because I didn't want to see the horror in my own eyes in case I spied people falling like bowling pins in our rearview.

Historically, from what I've been able to tell, there are not a lot of tourists in Naples, and if there *are* tourists, I contend that they are in da Michele, and they are in da Michele for the simple reason that they too have fallen for the hype that it's the birthplace of pizza (or at least one of). A couple of other Neapolitan pizzerias make the same claim, but still.

It's a thing. I mean, if you're serious about pizza, you go. If you love saucy carbs the way I do, claim to sweat flour like I do, well, then, you have no business not going. You can't bring shame on the Family, ya know? You simply have to walk the talk. Or on this occasion, drive the talk.

Even though there were a couple less-than-stellar moments on the road (going the wrong way on a one-way street and having to s-l-o-w-l-y back out of a narrow, dead-end alley while handsome, Southern Italian men with cigarettes mocked and chortled), John's driving was wildly impressive. There did come a point when our passage out of the alley had been crippled for so long that my bladder couldn't wait any longer—I had to pee so badly that when I saw the familiar Golden Arches nearby, I bailed out of the car without notice, offering only, "Sorry, I gotta go. If you're finished backing out before I'm back, call me on my cell and we'll meet up."

As I leapt from the car, I did catch a glance of John's *What the heck! You can't get out right here* face, but he said nothing and just kept inching in reverse while the men laughed and pointed (and, I found out later, eventually gave guidance). I felt awful for the guy, but when nature calls . . .

We did finally extricate ourselves from the quagmire and park the car in a jigsaw-puzzle parking lot that is down the street-ish from the pizzeria. As we walked along Corso Umberto to da Michele, I grabbed John's hand in a way that said I couldn't have been more impressed had he done brain surgery blindfolded, with no hands, on stilts, in a blizzard, backwards, on railroad tracks. As marvelous as his feat was, however, I may have been even more impressed with my own performance, having kept my pie-hole shut the entire time.

Now in the venerable, tiny pizzeria, we did what we do: I took photos of the blazing, 150-year-old, half-moon pizza oven (again); we got yelled at by the server more than once (again), who kept putting up his index finger and yelling in staccato, "I am ONLY ONE PERSON!"; and we ordered our two "normal" (per the wall menu) pizza pies: a no-frills marinara and a bare-bones margherita. Up to our naples in pizza, John ate three-fourths of his no-frills marinara, and I ate a fourth of my bare-bones margherita, leaving ourselves a whole pizza to take with us for further gluttony in the car on the next leg of our trip, our drive to Rome.

Preparing to say *Arrivederci*, I held our prized pie with one hand and stood at the door for the obligatory photo. On my right was the sole server who'd lambasted us for audaciously asking for beverages to go along with our pizzas. On my left was the ever-scowling Abe Vigoda look-alike who mans the cash register at the exit like an Italian bulldog (as if anyone would dare try to leave without paying their twelve euros).

With our top buttons undone on our respective pants, John and I waddled out of da Michele and down toward the busy corso. Just as we turned the corner, I noticed what appeared to be a mom and her tiny boy sitting on a mat in front of a store. The child—a stockier, Neapolitan version of little Ricky Ricardo—spotted us and our pizza box and, with his humongous chocolate, shining eyes and megawatt smile, bee-lined over to me and my da Michele prize, snagging it right out of my clutches. His movement was like poetry in motion, like Kobe Bryant at the basket. As his stealthy little olive hand reached for the box, he raised an eyebrow with a millisecond look of *permesso?* and then he snatched it, not waiting for *permesso*, in a pizza theft drive-by. It all happened so fast that, for a fraction of a fraction of a moment, I *almost* felt myself tug the box back before realizing, *Duh, of course this little boy needs my pizza pie much more than I do.*

As we passed mother and son, I felt John's hand tighten around mine and sensed his teary smile in concert with mine. It was a familiar moment of shared experience and empathy. We'd been down this road before; had many of these "incidents" over our thirty-three married years, when we both intuitively knew there was a bigger purpose, a greater point or need. Without words, we walked on the sidewalk alongside the cacophony and grit of a bustling, full-of-life, Neapolitan corso, toward our parked car, headed to Rome, hungry for more.

Liking

I'm not sure who said it first, since a few versions are floating around, but there's a variation attributed to author Paul Coelho, who supposedly said: "If everybody loves you, something is wrong. Find at least one enemy to keep you alert." I like to spin it this way: "If everyone likes you, you're not being real."

While it sounds good, I think that basic bit of wisdom is undervalued and underexercised. As a rule, we don't live it out. We tend to like being liked, so we *curb our enthusiasm*, to borrow the title from one of my favorite shows. For all his mischief and relational mayhem, "Larry David as Larry David" really seems to be the real deal in the HBO series. It's kind of perfect that he doesn't even have a fake name in the show. Like him or leave him, dude is integrated. I like him.

When I ride my bike, I perch my iPhone in a case on the top tube of my bike handles. This way I can hear it ring, and if I'm playing something audible, I can hear that too. On one of my regular routes through a nearby park, there are a lot of walkers. Sometimes I listen to sermons while I ride. I see the value in quiet rides, especially on mountain-bike trails, but on this route, I do like to multitask—listen and learn—although I *am*, sometimes, a tick self-conscious.

Passersby hear the sermons, and they turn to look. Occasionally they give me a knowing *I get you, girl* smile. More often I get a curious, *What the heck?* look. I don't play the sermons for anyone but me. Nevertheless,

I do wonder what people think. Will they judge my motives? Think I'm a Jesus freak, presuming to dictate what's best for them? This morning, as I rode up behind a woman who was walking, the preacher's volume went up as he said, "Know that God is there!" She craned her neck at that, and I just smiled.

I'm also aware that there are places in this world where I would be forbidden to do such a thing—even thrown in jail. On the hilly, IMA (International Medical Assistance) school driveway in Guatemala, a bruised and battered pick-up truck with a huge speaker on the rusty roof frequently and unabashedly blasts someone preach-yelling a sermon. It's done this way deliberately, to get attention and to deliver a message. I call it "Sermon on the Truck." Sometimes, when I ride my bike with my Bible lesson audibly playing, I think of that rusted-out truck sputtering up and down the Guatemalan hills, exhaling black exhaust, giving all it has to whomever will hear.

One morning on my ride through the park, I passed a couple of women walking in hijabs. I wondered, *Do they think I'm pedaling to proselytize?* Truth is, I'm just living my life. If, in the process of living my life, someone is inspired, cool.

Actor-comedian Tim Allen, when interviewed about his role on a family-friendly sitcom, said, "I think you should worry less about who you might offend and care more about who you might inspire." So, theoretically, there can be moments of unintentional inspiration, when we're just living our lives and focused on being real no matter who's listening or watching, with an air of "You do you; I'll do me." But I think there might be something even more integrated, more virtuous, more consequential, more deliberate. Such as fully embracing a specific message that, in all likelihood, *will* offend some, yet willingly risking our popularity because we recognize a higher value than being liked.

I find this to be tricky territory.

Another American actor comes to mind—and this one's been ostracized for his Christian beliefs. Like him or leave him, if you ask me, dude is integrated. He's living his life and willing to be flattened by the social Greyhound bus. It's as though he's voluntarily throwing himself under it.

Whether you agree with his positions or not, he's a big-picture seer, and how can you *not* respect him for that, even if you don't agree with his particular beliefs? He'd probably have a lot more Facebook likes, and a lot fewer people calling him names, if he'd stayed less "offensive." In our world of so-called tolerance, there's not much tolerance for Christians who stand by their faith when the details of their faith convictions are not popular.

In Eugene Peterson's *The Message* Bible, he paraphrases God's idea of integration, where we worry less, inspire more, and just plain stay real:

> You're blessed when your commitment to God provokes persecution. The persecution drives you even deeper into God's kingdom. Not only that—count yourselves blessed every time people put you down or throw you out or speak lies about you to discredit me. What it means is that the truth is too close for comfort and they are uncomfortable. You can be glad when that happens—give a cheer, even!—for though they don't like it, *I* do! And all heaven applauds. And know that you are in good company. My prophets and witnesses have always gotten into this kind of trouble (Matthew 5:10–12).

Reminds me of Inez and her friends at their assisted-living residence. I find that, as a general rule, those who are late in life are more genuine; they've gotten back to the basics.

If I'm honest, they can be a little rough around the edges there at the home. Yet it's hard to argue with their authenticity. There's something about it that's very innocent, very refreshing, very engaging—very childlike in a wonderful way.

Early on in life, we say it like we see it . . . until we see that, when we say it how we see it, people can get offended. So we learn to do life with a tweaked enthusiasm, adjusting the volume to comply with the opinions of others in mind. That's how we typically spend the bulk of our time here on earth too: moderated. But as we approach our latter days, something changes. I don't know whether people start to see the futility of being so careful, or whether they've just grown tired of the pretense, or whether their take-me-or-leave-me, you-don't-have-to-like-me air one day feels like a birthright they've been waiting to claim their entire life. But we need what they're bringing.

An image comes to mind of a ramshackle pick-up truck struggling up and down a hill, leaving a trail of black smoke like Morse code on its way to a not-so-distant kingdom. I see the bed of the truck filled with bouncing, guileless toddlers and seasoned seniors—two versions of the same people—living life the best way they know how, caring more about being genuine than being liked, delivering an unashamed message whose truth resounds toward an applauding heaven and comes to rest on the passersby below.

Aspirations of a Pipsqueak

It was a day I stayed home from church. Old enough to be home alone, but not too old to be wearing Raggedy Ann shorty pajamas, I was channel surfing while my family was at church. I don't recall the exact ailment. Maybe it was routine sniffles. Or it is also possible—more likely, actually—that I was pseudo-sick and getting an early start on the coming-down-with-something ploy. You see, pulling a sick-day Sunday would lay solid groundwork for a most credible Monday absence from school.

My plan fully employed, I planted myself in front of the big television in our den, probably with my *breakfast of Pampions* at my side: a stack of cinnamon toast and a tall Ovaltine.

Left to my own devices, and changing channels at whim, I watched entertaining televangelists whose theatrical high hair and clumpy mascara quite unexplainably sucked me in. And, I won't deny it, I liked what they said about a place way better than this one.

I eventually landed on some sort of lengthy call-to-action ad about sponsoring a child in what was then deemed "the third world," and I was overcome with sadness. The crying children had bloated, disproportionate bellies, and swarms of flies were landing on their faces, yet they didn't seem to have the energy to swat them away.

I'm all for churchgoing, but I learned early on: God sometimes speaks where and when we least expect it.

There was a radical, internal shift for me that day. I became slightly less naïve in my Raggedy Anns.

In one way I was shocked by the sight of these children, and in another, what I was seeing felt somehow familiar. On the outside, they looked like how I felt on the inside.

I remembered my mom telling me that when she brought me in as a foster child, my belly was distended, and the doctor said I was malnourished. So it's no wonder that I felt an overwhelming compulsion that demanded, *You can't just sit home and let this stuff go on, all comfy in your jammies with your cinnamon toast! You know now. You have to do something!* I also sensed that if I tried to help these kids, I'd be helping myself. So that day, I decided I wanted to be a *swooper*—someone who swoops in to help, someone like my mom and dad who swooped in to save me.

Forty or so years later, I don't know that I've done all that much swooping, or that anything of significance has changed in our world. Have we made a dent in poverty and hunger? We don't usually call it "the third world" anymore; we call it "the developing world," which, I think, is supposed to imply hope. *They* are in the process of developing (the implication being, I guess, that *we* here in the US have arrived, i.e., succeeded). And yet I know, without a doubt, that we in the States have not only *not* arrived, but in some ways, we have gone backwards.

My hunch is that the problem lies in the "them and us" mentality. *You be over there; I'll be over here.* I understand some of the logic of taking care of our own—you don't go down the street to feed your neighbor at the corner until you've fed your own kids in your own house—but still, aren't we all family?

Several years ago I was in a small study group with other Christians when the subject of homelessness came up, namely, those who panhandle. It was a casual, slowly unfolding conversation, but the group's consensus shocked me, making the jaw of my heart drop. The gist was all judgment, all *them* and *us*. I was embarrassed to call myself a Christian if that's what it means to be a Christian. (And I don't think it is.) I wanted to swat away the elitist tone. My snarky thought to them was, *Maybe you should stay home from church once in a while. Maybe you should get in front of the TV*

and watch some Sunday-morning, call-to-action infomercials, put down the
cinnamon toast, and go feed a malnourished pipsqueak just like me.

Martin Luther King Jr. said, "Use me, God. Show me how to take who I am, who I want to be, and what I can do, and use it for a purpose greater than myself." Left to our own devices, we see *them* and *us*; you over there, and me over here. We may look a little different on the outside, with different kinds of flies buzzing around us, and some of us may be a bit bloated with naiveté. But the reality is, it's just "US." We're all a little malnourished, one way or another, but with hopes of a place way better—here and over there.

It's Who You Know

Thanks to my husband, I have access (through his employer) to American Airlines' Admirals Club. I remember the first time John took me inside the elite, members-only club at Los Angeles International airport. I was suddenly privy to a secret, sleek lounge with couches, free-flowing free drinks, and salty, sugary snacks. *Ah, so this is how the other half lives!*

That's how we humans do. We create private-access clubs and exclusive societies. God, on the other hand, is no respecter of persons. He doesn't play favorites or show partiality to anyone because of their rank, status, wealth, beauty, smarts. Anything the world deems impressive, He's not so impressed. But we humans? We tend to categorize people. We organize them by their quality.

A "caste system" is a class structure determined by birth or heredity. In societies that abide by this system, you're born into either wealth or poverty and assigned a high or low status accordingly. You pretty much get put into a box and are expected to stay there.

Americans often associate a caste system with places like India, but it operates quietly elsewhere in the world. Consider England's royal family, for example. Prince Charles, the heir apparent, is hardly a free bird. The Prince of Wales was born into the position, and he can't undo it. Here in America, we have a caste system of sorts on our airplanes. It's divided by a teasing curtain that offers just enough view that you can see what you're missing—special drinks and snacks, warm cookies, warm towels. There *is* some wiggle room: You don't have to be dubbed *special* to sit in one of the luxurious seats. You can join if your wallet is fat enough to fund a first-class seat for your tush.

John and I have had the privilege of traveling to Europe several times now, and we're aware that we *can* make the torturous hours of intercontinental travel infinitely easier by upgrading to the front end of the plane for a *mere* 1,000-2,000 percent increase in our tickets. But we don't. We'd rather use our money eating our weight in tagliatelle when we get to Tuscany.

As we board our flight and head toward coach, we waddle through first class with our neck pillows tucked under our arms, looking longingly at the daybed seat compartments with all the fancy schmancy accoutrements. I try not to let my longing show, but I think my face probably betrays me.

On one episode of *Curb Your Enthusiasm*, Larry David gets into a bit of a kerfuffle with a fellow passenger on a plane. Larry, who has a prized seat on the pricey side of that sheer drape, finds that the restrooms designated for first class are occupied, so he heads to the 'hood, to coach. On the way, he is challenged by a woman who feels he is out of bounds (essentially, trespassing). An argument erupts, and Larry defends himself, yelling, "I'm coachy!" as if to say, "I'm humble like everyone else!"

From fiction to nonfiction:

On December 1, 1955, after a day of work for a Montgomery, Alabama, department store, Rosa Parks boarded the city bus to head home. She paid her fare and sat in an empty seat in the first row of back seats reserved for African Americans. These seats were directly behind the front-section seats reserved for Caucasian passengers.

As the bus traveled along its regular route, all of the white-only seats filled up. When the bus reached the third stop, several more white passengers boarded. Because some of them were now standing, the bus driver moved the "Colored"-section sign behind Parks and demanded that the four African Americans give up their seats so that the Caucasian passengers could sit. Three of them complied. When a black man sitting next to her gave up his seat, Parks moved, but only toward the window seat; she did not get up to move to the newly assigned Colored section. When the bus driver asked if she was going to stand up, Mrs. Parks said, "No, I'm not." Taken aback, the driver threatened, "If you don't stand up, I'm going to have to call the police and have you arrested," to which Rosa Parks said, "You may do that."

Rosa Parks's act of civil disobedience spoke loudly to a nation about its silent but treacherous caste system and was a catalyst for the civil rights movement.

In a way, I was born into a caste system of much smaller scale. As an orphan with a sketchy heritage, I was destined to remain in a box stamped in bold red letters: "Cole kid, aka Riffraff." Or so I thought.

The Bible reports a caste system even in Jesus's day:

> Later when Jesus was eating supper at Matthew's house with his close followers, a lot of disreputable characters came and joined them. When the Pharisees saw him keeping this kind of company, they had a fit, and lit into Jesus' followers. "What kind of example is this from your Teacher, acting cozy with crooks and riffraff?"
>
> Jesus, overhearing, shot back, "Who needs a doctor: the healthy or the sick? Go figure out what this Scripture means: 'I'm after mercy, not religion.' I'm here to invite outsiders, not coddle insiders" (Matthew 9:10–13 MSG).

Apparently, Jesus preferred hanging out with "riffraff" like me. The Pharisees, on the other hand—the yuckity yuck uppity ups—preferred the opposite. In their view, the disreputable characters they accused Jesus of spending time with were definitely not "the best and the brightest," the upper crust of society.

I've heard Pastor Greg Laurie's Bible-wide summary of this type of riffraff—his description of flawed people from Old Testament to New who suffered setbacks and made some royal mistakes, as well as unfortunates who had bad stuff happen or were simply prejudged like Rosa Parks. Here's Pastor Greg's rundown:

> Noah got drunk.
> Abraham was old.
> Jacob was a liar.
> Gideon was afraid.
> Rahab was a prostitute.
> Jeremiah and Timothy were too young.
> David had an affair and was a murderer.
> Elijah was suicidal.
> Jonah ran from God.
> Naomi was a widow.
> Job went bankrupt.
> John the Baptist ate bugs.
> Peter denied Christ.
> The disciples fell asleep while praying.
> The Samaritan woman was divorced more than once.
> Zacchaeus was too small.
> Timothy had ulcers.
> And Lazarus was dead.[16]

But of all the biblical accounts of societal cast-offs, there's one that is particularly encouraging. It starts with David, the "little guy who could."

He had made such a name for himself in battle against Goliath that he'd become the object of King Saul's seething jealousy and was forced

---

16 https://www.harvest.org/watch-and-listen/webcast/watch/gods-answers-to-mans-excuses

on the run to save his very life. King Saul's son Jonathan also happened to be David's best friend. As soon as Jonathan heard of his father's evil plot, he gave David a heads up, which allowed David a head start on his escape into the wilderness, where he hid for years, fleeing and fighting as needed.

Later on, when both King Saul and Jonathan were killed in a bloody battle with the Philistines, the conquering soldiers went looking for surviving members of the royal family so that they could annihilate any potential heirs. Jonathan's five-year old son, Mephibosheth, was rescued by his nanny, but during their dramatic escape, she accidentally dropped the boy and his feet were crushed, making it impossible for him to ever walk again.

Mephibosheth was taken to Lo-debar, a small town off the beaten path. Lo-debar was a logical choice for hiding someone, for who in their right mind would ever want to live there? It was a "box" of its own. The prefix *Lo* in Hebrew means "no, not, non, or never"; *debar* means "word, speak, say, tell, or utter." So Lo-debar was a place of "no word"—a place of inconsequence, insignificance. It was nothing to speak of.

Years later, David still thought often of his friend Jonathan and the solemn promise he had made the last time they had seen each other. Jonathan—who knew that David would be anointed as the future king of Israel—had requested that his friend remember his family and take care of them should anything ever happen to him. Wanting to honor that vow, David, who was now king, one day asked Ziba, Saul's former servant, "Is there anybody remaining in the family of Saul to whom I can show kindness for Jonathan's sake?"

Ziba told David about the disabled, orphaned Mephibosheth and that he had been living in lowly Lo-debar. David sent for his beloved friend's heir apparent. Likely traumatized from what had happened to him as a little boy, and having fearfully lived off the grid since then, Mephibosheth got belly down, face on the floor, before the king.

David called him by name.

Mephibosheth humbly answered, "Your servant."

"'Don't be afraid,' David said to him, 'for I will surely show you kindness for the sake of your father Jonathan. I will restore to you all the land that belonged to your grandfather Saul [the man who tried desperately to kill David], and you will always eat at my table'" (2 Samuel 9:7 NIV).

You will always eat at my table.

Free-flowing drinks. Salty and sugary snacks.

Mephibosheth could hardly believe his ears. Still bowing, he asked, "'What is your servant, that you should notice a dead dog like me?'" (2 Samuel 9:8).

I surmise from his response that Mephibosheth felt so much self-loathing and shame that he didn't see himself as an underdog. Instead, he considered himself as worthless as a *dead dog.*

David restored to Mephibosheth all that belonged to his father and grandfather, giving him every provision imaginable. Mephibosheth's life was suddenly headed on a northward trajectory. And everything changed. He went from poverty to wealth; from a life of obscurity and humiliation to the king's palace, even having a team of servants of his own.

Mephibosheth was now free to think outside of that box he'd been living in.

As children, some of us have been dropped, maybe even crushed. I was. I was also a child of the sixties, and I remember hearing the Creedence Clearwater Revival song "Lodi." I spent a majority of my childhood in an obscure little town not far from that slightly-less-obscure little town, and because I did, I know that even though the pronunciation is "Lo-die," it's close enough to "Lo-debar" to make a point.

In the song is the well-known line, "Oh Lord, stuck in Lodi again."[17] The song's backstory is about a struggling musician who's playing gigs and can't afford to get out of this one-horse, ho-hum, aggie town in California's

---

17 "Lodi," music and lyrics by John Fogerty (Fantasy, 1969).

Central Valley. He's stuck just far enough from the city lights of San Francisco that he can't quite raise the bus fare to get back there.

In Mephibosheth's case, he wasn't stuck *again* in Lo-debar, as much as *still*. He might sing, "Oh Lord, stuck in Lo-debar still."

I thought I was destined—forced into the back, in a box, in Lo-debar. A done, done deal. That was my perception for many years until I began to live my true heritage, not as rifraff but as *the best and the brightest,* simply because of Who I knew.

I'm in good company these days. I have an all-access pass to the Admirals Club. I went from my own version of lowly Lo-debar, and now I eat at the King's table. *And you are welcome too.*

Touched

After designating twelve disciples in Galilee and setting up His ministry, Jesus and His posse arrived in the town of Capernaum. Jesus had been teaching and healing many, and people were responding. I'm guessing some folks were just plain curious; some were looking to find fault and condemn Him; some were seeking a miracle; and others were eager to know and follow Him.

When a man covered in leprosy knelt before Him and asked to "become clean"—to have his horrible illness removed—Jesus could have accomplished this any way He wanted. He could have laser-beamed the healing through His God-eyes; pulled a *Look, Dad, no hands!* move; simply said the words "Be healed!"; or done something else altogether. But Jesus was touched by this man's faith, and so He reached out and touched *him.* He physically touched the highly contagious man with His own, unblemished hand. And the man was healed on the spot. Made clean.

Even though Jesus asked the newly healed, clear-skinned man to keep a lid on it, the man could not contain his excitement and told everyone within earshot about what Jesus had done for him. Like a celebrity unable to move about in town without the paparazzi, Jesus tried to take a little what we might call *me time,* but He was always found. Though He had the supernatural power to avoid the crowds entirely, He allowed himself to be found—to be touched—by the ailing and the seekers and the downcast.

When Jesus returned to Capernaum, the news spread like holy fire. As He was doing a little in-house preaching and teaching, five men—one of them flat on a stretcher, and four of them each holding up a corner—came to the maxed-out scene and saw that the doorway to this packed house was impassable. Other, less-tenacious types might have deemed this an impossible situation, but these men looked up. The ingenuity and doggedness of the paralyzed man's friends is one of my favorite parts of this short story about persistence and faith. They were Little Engines That Could in their own right.

Somehow, some way, they got their buddy up on the roof, dug out a hole directly above where Jesus was teaching, and lowered the guy down through the ceiling so that he was smack dab in front of the Teacher-Preacher-Healer. Jesus, so impressed by their collective faith, said to the man on the stretcher, "Son, I forgive you." Jesus knew the condemners in His audience would call what He'd done "blasphemy" since, in their line of thinking, God and only God can forgive sins. Bummer for them, *He was God.*

Jesus queried the religious know-it-alls: "What's easier? To say, 'I forgive your sins,' or 'Get up and walk?'" The clear implication was that it would be easier to do a physical healing than a spiritual one. To clarify for the skeptics and judgers that He had the authority and power to do both, He did. Jesus commanded the man to get up, pick up his stretcher, and go on home. The man did just that—he got up, picked up the stretcher, and, like Elvis, he left the building. And those in the crowd who were just plain curious, those looking to find fault and condemn, those seeking a miracle, and those who were eager to know and follow Jesus were all Godsmacked.

If you read through the Gospels—Matthew, Mark, Luke, and John—you get a picture of the kinds of people who were attracted to Jesus. Sure, everyone was invited—the poor, the rich, the somebodies, the nobodies, the religious, the irreligious, the white collar and the blue collar, the women and the men, the sick, the healthy, the bosses and the servants, the homeless and the homeowners . . . There were no privileged members in Jesus's potential posse. It seems to me, though, that Jesus did have a certain demographic in mind, a target audience. He came to bring healing to the endangered among our species—those with sick, broken bodies and minds.

If you really think about it, that covers a whole lot of people, if not everyone. The man in a Brioni suit sitting in a temperature-controlled Maserati at the bottom of the four-level interchange off-ramp in downtown Los Angeles is no different than the man selling bags of oranges on the curb inches from him in the blazing summer sun. Their illnesses might look a little different on the outside, but to the One who sees men's hearts, brokenness is brokenness.

Jesus healed lepers, servants, sick mothers, the blind, the demonized, the paralyzed; He even raised the dead. If you read through the biblical accounts of Jesus's earthly ministry, you may see a pattern: certain types accepted Him. It tended to be the ragamuffins, the visibly messy ones, the underdogs, the bullied ones—people we might call the Nobodies, the Unimportant, the Unpopular, the Uncool Kids, the Offramp Orange Peddlers, Those with Nothing Left to Lose, and those Little Lovers Who Believed They Could, Simply Because They Knew He Could.

Next, pay attention to the ones who were threatened or offended by Him and who ultimately rejected Him: the Know-It-Alls, the Smarty-Pants, the Religious, the Sticklers, the Educated, the Rule-Keepers, the In-the-Box-Thinkers, the Color-Inside-the-Liners.

There's a good bit of proof in Scripture that Jesus was deeply touched by *and acted according to* people's faith. He healed one woman simply because He knew that she'd reached out in faith and touched the hem of His robe as He passed by.

We're all in earshot. Jesus is passing by. Will you reach out and touch Him? Will you let Him touch *you*?

As a little girl in church, I had a few favorite old-timey hymns that I'd belt out. Hands down, my fave was and still is "Amazing Grace." "Blessed Assurance" was also a winner, and then, rounding out my top three, was "He Touched Me," written by Bill Gaither and recorded not only by his trio but by many others, including cool-kid-who-left-the-building Elvis.[18]

Even when I didn't understand why, those songs made me cry. Maybe because I was fully aware of the leprosy on my insides, and I wanted to be made clean. And maybe because, in God's amazing grace, I was touched by the Healer who allows Himself to be found.

---

18 Check out the lyrics at https://genius.com/Gaither-vocal-band-he-touched-me-lyrics

Little Love to Biggest Love

This much I know for sure: I was born at General Hospital. As in the soap opera. That building is my literal birthplace. I have documentation. Many other things about my birth and earliest childhood, however, are a mystery.

My birth certificate doesn't say how much I weighed at birth. It's not that the space is blank; it's that there's not even a space. In the single, earliest photo I've seen of myself, I look to be about twelve months old. My sister Beth and some unknown little boy are proudly holding me up as though I hadn't gotten my sea legs yet. I'm wearing faded denim overalls, Little Rascals style.

For my entire life, I've passed by LA's mammoth County Hospital, which is downtown and clearly visible from the 5 Freeway. Since I was a little girl, I've stared at that building as long as my neck would stretch, hoping that somehow, by osmosis, I'd glean more information—maybe get some blanks filled in—just by looking at it.

Because of the mystique that formidable building holds in my life story, I've made some assumptions over the years. For one, I've presumed the hospital is a normal, hustling, bustling medical center—with blood and surgeries and babies and an ER and intercoms and lousy, rubbery cafeteria pizza.

Last year on my birthday, I told John I wanted to go on a nostalgic little adventure. I wanted to investigate my birthplace—go walk the halls, breathe the air, see what we see, maybe discover something germane about my birth day. We parked the car and aimed our feet toward the familiar-from-a-distance main entrance, bypassing a massive new structure. As we approached, we saw that it was decorated in welcoming, festive balloons and colorful ribbons. It looked a little like a job fair, or maybe someone's birthday party. *Hmmmmmm.* As we began our ascent up the concrete staircase that would take us inside the building, we saw a sign that said "The Wellness Center. *Bienvenidos. Su centro para la salud y el bienestar,*" which translates to "Welcome. Your center for health and wellness." Making our way into the Art Deco foyer, our eyes were immediately drawn to the glorious art above. The domed ceiling depicted some of history's great physicians.

Past the ornate interior doors we found a glossy, spic-and-span hallway set up with more balloons and tables, with clusters of friendly faced people operating what looked to be a temporary free clinic. On our right, away from the activity, we noticed a handwritten sign haphazardly taped to the elevator that essentially said, *Do not pass Go.* After pushing the elevator button to check the sign's veracity, John pointed to the alternative: a door down a different, unmanned hall with a permanent, official-looking sign that said "Stairwell."

"Wanna go up?" he mouthed.

"Sure," I said. I came for adventure.

What we found was something out of *28 Days Later* or any other creepy, apocalyptic film. I hadn't seen this coming. Ignoring every closed door and Keep Out sign, we climbed each floor higher and higher, breathing the stale air, wandering through the maze of eerie, surreal halls with peeling walls. It literally looked like a bomb had gone off—faded, warped, and broken desks overturned; dusty rotary phones with receivers hanging by their curly cords; file drawers pulled out, exposing private patient files, admission records, and medical charts; papers strewn like confetti. Medical books were dumped everywhere. Every kind of hospital equipment imaginable was littering the space—shattered light boxes, syringes and clamps, forceps and scissors and trimmers and suction tubes and surgical knives and hypodermic needles, banged-up white boards, open lockers with their contents dumped, hospital beds and steel bedframes. There were also numerous doors hanging on hinges, broken windows, and a lone wheelchair sitting dead center in this horror-film hallway. We saw dirt-caked bathtubs and sinks, rooms covered in soot, ceiling tiles on mysteriously wet floors, bird droppings and rat holes, walls covered in mold and all shades of fade. And yellow police tape.

Finally, we made it to roof access. Alongside the pigeons, we inched up on our tippy toes to look out at the horizon, and John even gave me a foot up as I climbed a little farther on the outer wall. Peering out through the stone cut-outs from this forgotten-world paradigm, I could see Los Angeles fully alive—the wispy clouds over sundrenched, sky-scraping buildings, multilevel freeways and miniature cars, houses and apartments and schools and parking lots, the Golden Arches and palm trees, maybe a movie studio or two, and foothills backed up by the San Gabriel Mountain range. Just across the street below us, a beautiful green park was teeming with teeny people walking around the Lincoln Heights neighborhood, just doing their day.

It wasn't anything like I'd imagined. We'd climbed eighteen flights (the nineteenth was locked), skulked around each floor like intrigued, drop-jawed zombies. My birthplace, now defunct, lay in utter ruin.

After I got home, I did a bit of online research and learned that the Depression-era structure had been given the nickname "The Great Stone Mother." *Perfect.* Built in the early 1920s, the historic monolith with its eighty-ton façade has twenty stories and covers a million square feet of space. Back in its day, it had a jail ward—on the thirteenth floor, no less. The best bit of trivia I discovered was that the iconic beauty, Marilyn Monroe, was also born at The Great Stone Mother. Norma Jean was born in 1923 in the charity unit, which is most likely where I'd have been born had the unit been operative thirty-nine years later.

I guess we were both charity cases.

The beginning of the end of this structure as an operational hospital began after the 6.7 San Fernando Valley earthquake in 1994, which caused widespread damage throughout LA and renewed concerns about building safety and codes, especially in hospitals. A new earthquake law was enacted soon after, which forced retirement of the aging building. In its place (next door-ish), the county built the $1 billion complex—the massive new structure we'd bypassed. I guess the whole kit and caboodle is now known as Los Angeles County/USC Medical Center, including my old, raggedy, historical birthplace.

Some of my friends have done water births, delivering their babies in a livestock trough (what looks like a large, metal bathtub). Some have given birth in a regular bathtub, and some in an inflatable wading pool. I've given birth to one of my babies in a town called Placentia, which I think is hilarious. My friend Jen was born on New Year's Eve 1972 in a purple Dodge Demon in Pontiac, Michigan. (Sure, it would have been great if it had been an actual Pontiac, but not greater than a purple Dodge Demon. C'mon.) Jen basically fell out of her mom's mumu. My friend Kirsten was born at the Salvation Army Home for Unwed Mothers in Oakland, California. John's grandma Elizabeth delivered Sandy, John's mom, on an ironing board with a drunk doctor attending.

All this to say: some of us haven't had the most auspicious births or birthplaces. Then again, Jesus didn't either.

First, God the Father chose two unknowns—two peasant teenagers from tiny, bumpkin Nazareth—and gave them a mind-bending assignment. The angel first came to Mary, a virgin, and told her that she would become pregnant, but she would not be making this baby with her betrothed, Joseph. No, this would be an immaculate conception. The Spirit of God would miraculously hover over her, and the resulting embryo growing inside her would be a *deity*: God with wrinkly baby skin on. Her child would be both fully man and fully God. She would deliver a son, who in turn would deliver her. And by the way, the angel said, this was God's rescue plan for the world.

We don't know a whole lot about Jesus's human birth. We don't know how much He weighed, even though He would carry the weight of the world. But we do know some of the basics; among them, that He was born in Bethlehem in paltry, earthly accommodations—a manger, no less. An ancient livestock trough.

We don't know what color His eyes were or if He was a bald baby or if He was a fussy eater or a good sleeper or if He sucked His thumb. We know that while His name was Jesus, He had many titles, including "Immanuel," which is one of my personal favorites. Isaiah had prophesied seven hundred years earlier: "She will give birth to a son and will call him Immanuel (which means 'God with us')" (Isaiah 7:14).

Jesus was not just God's Son. He was God. I know, it's a hard thing to wrap a brain around. Truth is, for some, this leap of faith is a smidgen too far. But whatever a person has decided about Jesus, they ought to consider this factual tidbit: the event of His birth would forever divide human time as we know it, BC and AD. So there's that.

The preacher Charles Spurgeon described Jesus this way: "Infinite and an infant. Eternal and yet born of a woman. Almighty, and yet nursing at a woman's breast. Supporting a universe, and yet needing to be carried in a mother's arms. Heir of all things, and yet the carpenter's despised son."

I love the art of story. In my opinion, the best story is one that includes a twist you never saw coming. Jen's Dodge Demon story, for one. I bet Jen's parents did *not* see that coming.

I think the story of Jesus is truly the most dramatic, most theatrically delicious, greatest story ever told, partly because it's the twistiest. No matter how much they were let in on what was going to happen, Jesus's followers just didn't get it—they did not see what was coming.

Granted, they knew He was the Messiah, but they thought that meant He would reign as a victorious military king who would rescue the Israelites from the Romans. They expected Him to wield His power through miracles and maybe massacre.

Jesus's plan was to be king, yes, but Jesus's kingdom would come about a little differently, and it would look a little different than anyone imagined. (Okay, *a lot* different.) Rather than ruling by force, Jesus came to fulfill the Old Testament prophecies that said He would be the suffering Servant-King. He would be the sacrificial lamb who would die for the sins of all people and bring God's rule to earth by giving up His life on the cross.

After His agonizing and very public death, Jesus's family and followers were devastated—as if a bomb had gone off in their hearts. To them, all seemed pointless and lost. Yet that was *not* the end of the story. The biggest twist was yet to come, what I call the Ultimate Jaw-Dropper.

As a mom myself, I try and imagine what it must have been like for Mary to watch her son be beaten nearly beyond recognition, nailed to a cross, and die an unjust, agonizing death, unable to do anything to change what was happening. I imagine she felt like she was dying. This was the tiny baby she'd nursed and held, propped up until he got his legs under him. This was the little boy she'd caught when he fell taking his first steps; the child she'd cried over, dreamed with, prayed for, loved with her whole mom heart. This son whom God had given through her very being was the same one she'd swaddled in rags and tucked into a humble manger, and tucked into her life.

No one, not even Jesus's mom, got it until they got it. But when they did, everything was changed. If it was hard for Jesus's eyewitnesses to wrap their brains around what was happening—who He was—it's not hard for me to imagine why we have such a hard time without His physical presence. Still, there is another presence available to us. But we have to want it.

He has wrapped His truth and His heart around those who will believe in Him. No matter the state of our lives—whether they're in disarray as that historic hospital was, or whether we've pretty successfully kept that ground floor spic-and-span, where no one would ever mistake us for a rag-amuffin or a charity case—the mystery begins to unfold the farther in we go, as we climb higher and higher, headed for the roof-top view.

Angel's Wink

'm what you might call "wink-challenged," medically known as Awkward Wink. While I do get a nice little tingle when someone winks at me, I am physically unable to return the favor. Believe me, I've tried. But I get nervous and freeze up. The best I've been able to do is a p a i n f u l l y s l o o w-motion wink.

Even though I have wink-envy, I have been a wildly blessed wink recipient. There are the traditional, physical winks, and there are other types—other manifestations, if you will . . .

We had walked into the Bakersfield In-N-Out burger restaurant, and there was literally ONE person in line. I thought to myself, *Self, take note. This has never happened in your In-N-Out eating career.* I scouted out a booth while John ordered (he knows what I like). John brought our Cokes to the table and excused himself to the little boys' room while I waited for our burgs and fries. Through the window across the restaurant, I saw a pair of Greyhound buses pull up, which then proceeded to dump out about a million people, all of whom had to wait in line. And wait. And wait. I sat there, not exactly smug, but admittedly relieved, as if an angel had looked down and given us a little "I got this one for you today, guys" wink.

While I've had a richly blessed life so far, I've also had some days, and even seasons (if I'm completely honest), where I haven't felt very winked upon. "Wink shortages." In general lately, it's felt a little like that. So the

In-N-Out wink was a nice touch. A nice reminder of what's big-picture true.

The reason for our Bakersfield pitstop was another reminder that, even during those seemingly winkless seasons, there is a greater reality—something always to be grateful for. John and I had just spent the weekend at my parents' place in Northern California, and during this weekend, my mom had winked at me more than once. She's one of those long-timers who's getting sweeter with age. I've found the "disposition of aging" can go either way, and my mom's going the sweet route.

For my purpose here, I'm going to propose that a "wink" is *grace*. Grace can be defined as unmerited favor—a blessing or good fortune bestowed on us without having done anything to earn it. It's not luck; not "good timing"; not "right place, right time," even though it can feel like any of those. It's a sweet glance from heaven.

When I was a toddler, an angel winked at me and gave me a mom—a mother who knew exactly what it was to love a child long and well. Technically, she isn't a supernatural angel, but in my eyes, she's the closest thing to it. The woman is a natural—and the finest, most graceful of winkers.

Bully for You

*"Do I not destroy my enemies
when I make them my friends?"*

–ABRAHAM LINCOLN

As far back as the seventeenth century, the word *bully* commonly referred to something good.

"Hey, guess what?! I got a promotion at work!"
"Bully for you!"
"My daughter just found out she's been accepted to medical school."
"Well, bully for her!"

Now, though, we hear the word *bully* and we think of the movie *Mean Girls* or, more recently, *Thirteen Reasons Why*. Or we wonder what terrible, real-life news story we'll hear next, where one child (or children) intimidated another into the unthinkable, or a student was so horribly bullied that he or she took revenge on the whole school, bringing guns and shooting the place up. Sometimes bullying is mentioned in tandem with cyberspace, where the battlefield is even more toxic and limitless.

Kelly was mainstreamed into Fair Oaks Elementary School, and the first person I'd ever seen bullied. She had special needs and was in a wheelchair. Kelly was routinely taunted and teased at school. I would sit with her sometimes and talk to her, but I never stood up for her, never told the bullies to back off. I never really allied myself with Kelly in a way that put myself on the line for her. If I had, maybe I could have helped her, showed her she wasn't alone. But I was intimidated by the crowd.

My experience with *being* bullied pales in comparison to what Kelly endured. The first time I was bullied was by Tonya, a towhead in third grade. I don't know why she wanted to give me a beatdown. But I was able to dissuade her from doing so by appealing to her humanity (and also whistling in the dark, aka "faking it till I made it"). The next time I was bullied was three years later, by Claudia, in sixth grade. She had a bit of a gang following, and so things were a little more involved and precarious. It took a few "whistling conversations" before I could talk her and her people out of beating me up after school.

I don't know why Tonya or Claudia wanted to hurt me, but I was really afraid.

Probably the scariest bullying incident for me was at Knott's Berry Farm amusement park with my friend Cheryl. We were thirteen or fourteen years old and had been dropped off for the day by Cheryl's mom. For no apparent reason, a pack of older, bigger girls decided to terrorize us for the afternoon. There too I whistle-talked my/our way out of it, appealing to those girls' higher, better selves. (You're welcome, Cheryl. Don't mention it.)

Nick Vujicic really knows what it is to be bullied. Nick rolls out in his wheelchair onto a high school gymnasium floor packed with students in El Centro, California. Before he gets to the center circle, he begins talking, wasting no time in addressing what his listeners are probably all wondering.

"I was born this way," he tells them. "There's no medical reason for why this happened. My brother and sister were both born with arms and legs. Sometimes things happen in life that don't make sense . . ."

When he was younger, Nick was a popular target for bullies. Typically, when he would enter a room, it would take about three seconds before someone would start in on him. Literally, three seconds.

You'd think maybe bullies would have standards and not stoop so low as to tease someone like him. But they declared open season on Nick. And at eight years old, he "started to die," he says, because he began to believe the bullies' lies. It got so bad that he looked at himself one day, and then looked at everyone else, and he saw that everyone else had more than he had. He asked, "Why? Why me?" but no one had answers. Not his doctors, not his parents. His parents loved him like crazy, encouraged him so much, told him that he was beautiful just as he was. But still, the voices of the bullies were drowning out everything good and true, and Nick wanted to die.

Adult Nick points to a Bible next to him on a table in the center of the gymnasium and tells the students, "This is my favorite book because it shows me my full potential here on earth."

Eight-year-old Nick somehow chose to stop believing the lies from the bullies and instead focused on the truth his parents had always told him—the truth he found in his favorite book: that he had value, purpose, a destiny.

When Nick was thirteen, a seventeen-year-old had been bullying him for three weeks. Craning his neck to look up at the six-foot-tall aggressor from his wheelchair, Nick said, "Hey, can you please stop it?"

"Stop what?"

"Stop teasing me."

"What are you talking about?"

"Every time I pass by, you say that stuff."

"What stuff?"

I'm guessing the bully played dumb because he was a bit taken aback by Nick's courage to confront him directly. Nick continued, "I want you to stop. I forgive you, but stop it."

In a mocking tone, the bully asked, "Awww, is that hurting you?"

Nick could have said "Nah" or he could have said "Yeah." It takes a level of humility to admit that somebody's words or actions are hurting you. Nick admitted it.

The bully seemed penetrated by Nick's honesty and said, "All right, I'm sorry, man. You know I was just playing around." And then Nick asked the guy for a hug, and the two of them hugged it out.

Nick chose to be honest about how the teasing was hurting him, and this time, his appeal to the bully's humanity worked.

We have a list of banned phrases in our house. One of them for John is, "I'm done rubbing your feet, Pammy." Another is, "I was just being playful."

Thankfully, I recognized the pattern earlier rather than later. John would do or say something that I felt had crossed a line, and when I told him it made me feel bad, he'd blow it off by saying, "It's okay; I was just being playful." (Queue record-scratch sound effect.)

Once when I was at sixth-grade science camp, I was lying on the top bunk, chatting with my roommate, who was on her bunk below me. Without warning, this girl pushed her feet hard into the underside of my mattress, which ejected me from my bed like a jack-in-the-box. I was catapulted into the air and landed flat on my back onto the hardwood floor of our cabin. This knocked the wind out of me, and I was unable to move for several minutes. Thank God that was the physical extent of it, but what lingered was the feeling of being so betrayed by my friend, who not only didn't apologize but who thought it was funny. *Yeah, good one.*

Another time in elementary school, I was at my turn at the water fountain when my friend behind me gave me a friendly little shove from behind, which pushed me into the faucet, which chipped my front tooth. She was being playful too.

The bunk flipper, the tooth chipper, and John "I was just being playful" Capone were caught up in their own amusement and didn't intend to hurt me. But I was hurt just the same.

There are pages upon pages of anti-bullying strategies online, and many include some variation of these tips:

1. Ignore the bully. Just walk on by.
2. Stand up for yourself. Show the bully you can't be intimidated. Be Teflon.
3. Don't bully back. Be better than the bully. Model by example.
4. Don't let your feelings show.
5. Tell an adult. Get support from someone in authority who will have your back.

I imagine that, throughout Nick's life, he tried all of the above, and maybe some things worked at different times. Still, by eight years old, he wanted to die.

In the example he shared at the gym in El Centro, he bypassed number four from the list above and did, in fact, show his feelings. In many contexts—sports, politics, war—revealing "weakness" can be deadly. If your opponent sees it, he or she can exploit that soft spot. Capitalize on it. Use it to advantage. I would argue that Nick didn't display weakness by showing his feelings; he revealed his strength. Rather than whistling in the dark, Nick got in the bully's face a little about his broken heart. And the bully was moved by it.

It's a no-brainer why bullies bully. Born from copycat behavior, jealousy, or a core insecurity, a bully's desire to feel better or to elevate himself morphs into hurtful behavior that tries to diminish someone else. Just think of how far bullying can go. Hitler was one of the most horrific bullies in history. He tormented an entire race and did his best to wipe them out by genocide.

Bullying has been around since forever, and there are countless stories of it in a book as old as the Bible (Joseph's bullying brothers, for example, or the taunting bully Goliath). Maybe all evil comes from a bully.

In our most recent presidential election, we saw some of the worst of bullying in politics. People who ought to know better and be better, weren't. Our children were watching, are watching, and I'm horrified at the short- and long-term effects when our highest elected officials behave like playground bullies. What will our children think? Who will our children emulate?

In the gut-punching 2011 documentary *Bully*, two moments take the wind out of me. One is early in the film when a teeny boy, Cody, is being comforted by the school principal, and she asks him how it makes him feel when he's called names. I expect a one-word answer: "Sad." Instead, he responds: "It breaks my heart."

And that broke my heart.

About midway through the film comes the other moment that jumps off the screen. Alex is one of the teens featured in the film, and the target of merciless torment. With the camera on him, he lists some of the ways others bully him. He says, "They punch me in the jaw . . . strangle me . . . knock things out of my hand . . . take things from me . . . sit on me . . ." And, he says, "They push me so far that I want to become the bully."

That is the insidious, often-contagious nature of bullying. Frequently, children who are bullied repeat the hurtful behavior themselves.

When I was a child, a kid who was being bullied was often offered this reminder by a well-meaning adult: "Sticks and stones may break your bones, but names can never hurt you." Even as a kid, I knew that was a complete load of crap. Of course names and words hurt. Maybe they hurt worst of all.

We tell our children to "use your words" instead of hands for fighting back, but what about when people use their words to hit?

If I could go back to grade school, I think I would not only sit with Kelly but I'd speak up for her. Kelly was unable to speak because of her developmental disability. I was unable to speak because of my fear disability.

If I had a redo, I'd appeal to the bullies' humanity, to their heart. I'd open up mine and ask them to open up theirs. When Nick spoke forthrightly to that seventeen-year-old bully, he not only asked him to stop bullying him because it was hurting him; he told him that he forgave him.

After Joseph's jealous brothers had bullied and betrayed him, thrown him into a pit, and sold him into slavery, he did not repay them in kind. He changed things up. He reversed direction, blazed a new trail, turned the tide, set a new tone and a new standard—he opened his heart to them. He disarmed them with his honesty. He told them, "What you meant for evil, God meant for good" (Genesis 50:20, paraphrase). He let them see his very real tears—and he forgave them.

Bully for us when we turn evil on its head by standing with the underdog. Hugging it out, not slugging it out. Opening our hearts and using our voice. Bully for us when we destroy our enemies by making them our friends.

Anonymous

"We are breathing egos acting
like we aren't a speck of dust
on a speck of dust in outer space."

—SARAH SILVERMAN

A husband and a wife walk into a diner. They enjoy a nice, simple meal. The husband pulls out his wallet to pay the check, and the wife suggests that they leave a disproportionately large cash tip. Just for fun. Just for the love of it. As they walk out of the diner, the husband proposes that they stop and peek through the window to see the server's reaction when she finds the tip. The wife disagrees. "No," she says. "If we do that, we get something out of it."

This was many years ago, and every once in a while they still do their version of the dine-and-dash, never looking back.

Jesus told His disciples to check their motives, make sure they're pure: "Be careful not to practice your righteousness in front of others to be seen by them. If you do, you will have no reward from your Father in heaven" (Matthew 6:1 NIV). My interpretation: "Check yourself before you wreck yourself."

Whether we admit it or not, we're all minuscule bits of dust inclined to want a little glory, a little payoff. We're prone to look back in through the diner window and, to quote Bill Murray in *Caddyshack*, get "a little somethin' for the effort."

Motives can be such tricky little buggers. Even while doing good, big-hearted, heavenly work, our motives can be mixed, with impure ones sneaking in. Even the finest spiritual gangstas sometimes have to contend with the temptation to feed the ego.

I was privileged to sit with a twice-widowed mother of eleven (two by natural birth) this past week who is a spiritual gangsta. As I sat and listened to Margaret's story, I was stunned by her high-cheekboned beauty, her energy, her resilience, her dedication, her independence, her work ethic, her honesty, and mostly, her fierce love. She laughed when I told her that she is a "tenacious lover on steroids." If this book had a mascot, it could be Margaret.

I wanted to meet Margaret after her daughter Anna told me about their family. I needed to meet this woman who'd taken in nine underdogs—castaways, all with varying degrees of disability; some quite drastic, and some terribly ill. Nearly all were from international orphanages, and many from unspeakable conditions, such as the child who was literally left abandoned in an orphanage after the 1988 Armenian earthquake that killed fifty thousand people. Or the baby who was so dehydrated he couldn't cry.

Many times over, Margaret literally saved these children's lives. Several of them, like Anna, were wasting away, on the verge of death if they didn't receive medical treatment and tenacious love STAT. None of the children came through any planned process. "They just appear," she remarks. "Then I say yes and I figure out a way to get them out of their country and adopt them . . . . When God gives you an assignment, you say yes."

She describes her first adoption. She'd been recently widowed and was in a foreign country along with her two biological children. She had just begun her new job of establishing a nonprofit when her son came home from his volunteer work at a rehab and said, "There's this child there, and *you HAVE to adopt her.* She's missing a leg . . . and she's not going to get an education . . . and she's just adorable and smart and . . . and . . . and . . ."

At first Margaret told her son no. He pressed her: "Let me take you to meet this little girl at least."

Margaret says she took one look at the child and said, "Sure, what do I need to do?"

This would come to be the way it would work every time a child was presented to her. "Once I met the child," she says, "it was always, 'Sure, what do I need to do?'" She repeats the line as she describes the other adoption experiences, and every time she says it, she chuckles—almost as if she "couldn't help but help."

If Margaret wasn't taking in children herself, she was being asked if she knew of someone who might be interested, what with all her contacts. Like the time social services was working with a young pregnant woman. They asked if Margaret would keep her eyes open for a family, and so she did. She looked. The months passed, the child was born, and Margaret says, "Nobody showed up." So Margaret showed up—she adopted the child herself.

Her eyes were open; her heart was open. There were children she was advised against taking, told that they would not survive. "Too much pain," she was warned. She took them anyway, and she loved them back to life. Like Anton, one of three children still at home today.

A social worker from Eastern Europe had called and said, "I'm sending you a picture, and I need you to put it on your computer screen. The child is headed to a warehouse where they will not feed him and he will die. *Because that's what they do with kids like this.* His mother was exposed to Chernobyl's radiation. He only has an arm . . . he's just your basic, orthopedic kid!" (I asked her to clarify what that meant, and she said that he was *perfect*, except that he was a triple amputee.)

Margaret's good friend happened to walk by and see the photo and asked her, "Who is that angel? That boy is beautiful!" To which Margaret chuckled and remarked, "I don't know, but I think I'm about to adopt him!"

Margaret says she didn't even ask her family what they thought about it; she flew to the orphanage in Eastern Europe and met the two-year-old. The social services people working with Margaret on her home study advised her against taking Anton. "Too many reasons why it's a bad idea," they said. Margaret told them, "Nah, I'm taking him. He's just your basic, orthopedic kid."

Today Anton thrives, having beaten all the impossible odds. He's done public speaking in front of thousands. She says, "He's fearless; he can do anything. He's been a gift."

Anton is at the same college as Anna and *coincidentally* "strolled by" in his wheelchair the day I met Anna. I was lucky enough to get a hug.

People naturally notice Anna. Anna is a beautiful girl who looks a little different. I think she'd be amazing for the Dove Real Beauty campaign, the ads featuring those with unconventional, under-appreciated beauty. Anna was born with hydrocele, which means part of her brain was on the outside of her skull, exposed and resting on her forehead. Along with hydrocele, she had frontal nasal dysplasia.

Born in Eastern Europe, Anna was placed in an orphanage by her biological parents when she was three days old. Margaret first heard about the little girl when Anna was six years old. A friend called Margaret and said that Anna would die soon if she didn't receive help. Doctors had placed titanium plates in her head to sort of hold things together at age three, but now it was all deteriorating and Anna was dying. So Margaret flew across the world to meet Anna, adopted her, and got Anna the surgeries that would rebuild her skull. Meanwhile, Margaret built her a life.

Today Anna is in her first year of college taking general education courses, with plans to transfer at some point to a school with a culinary program. She loves cooking and baking, has a job working with children after school, volunteers at her mom's nonprofit. She also sings like an angel, writes her own music, plays guitar and piano, and excels at athletics—soccer, basketball, track, and cross-country are her sports.

When I asked Anna who some of her heroes are, she said her mom. She's watched her mom work many years for a large nonprofit that comes alongside those who are hurting and gives relief. Clearly, Margaret's entire life—at home and work, day and night—has been about swooping in and saving lives. But when I asked Anna's mom what motivates her to do what she does, saving lives is not really what Margaret talked about most. Instead, she revealed a personal side that people with false modesty deny or deflect. I was blown away by her honesty.

When Margaret was, as she puts it, "several adoptions in," a social worker with seven adopted children of her own warned Margaret of something she'd witnessed many times over and personally experienced herself. The woman said, "It may not mean anything to you now, but someday it will. For some people, adopting multiple children can become an addiction. I can testify to that. You get a lot of ego support for what you do. People tell you how wonderful you are; they call you a saint; they give you a lot of reinforcement. You have the excitement of the travel and meeting the child, and it's kind of a high. And then things become routine and ordinary and you are going to want that high again."

Margaret shared another conversation with me, this one with a woman who had adopted eight Ethiopian children. Margaret says the adoptive mother was a great woman of faith who ended up being a real friend and spiritual guide to her. This woman suggested that they both need to honestly ask themselves on a continual basis, "Are we really doing God's work, or are we trying to make ourselves feel important?" (Hence the Sarah Silverman "breathing egos" quote.)

Like the apostle Paul in 2 Corinthians 12:9, Margaret "boasted of her weakness," confessing to me that she has quietly struggled with this over the years. In her career with the nonprofit, the company has moved her all around the country—and sometimes out of the country—in what we might call flukes or happy accidents, but what are probably, in reality, providence and divine orchestration. Now, though, for the past eight years, she finds herself dwelling in what she calls a "reticent culture" on the East Coast: in all that time, no one has asked her about her children, where they came from, why she adopted them, nothing. Margaret said I am the first person who's asked her anything about her family or background for that long.

In a way, she is almost baffled by this quirky disinterest, but deep down she knows that's exactly why she's here. She believes God orchestrated this very move for that very reason: He removed the possibility of her ego being fed the way it had been for so many years. He knew this was a danger zone, so He moved her to a different time zone for her own good. (Personally, I think He wants to reward her big-time in heaven. Enough with these paltry accolades of Planet Earth.)

"I ask myself every day," Margaret said, "whether I am really doing God's work or doing something to feel important. I had elements of altruism clear back to my childhood, but over the years, I got caught up in this ego boost."

I videotaped our chat that day and, watching the playback now, I notice things I missed then, when I was sitting across from her at a table. Subtler things such as the look in Margaret's eyes when she's transported back to those life-making moments: the first meeting with a child who was withering, recalling a time of tragedy and confusion while raising kids with special needs, or the instant she lit up as she talked about Anna's beauty, meaning it with all her heart when she sweetly nodded and said, "She's a beautiful girl."

I imagine it's much the way our heavenly Father's face lights up as he sees past our surface to what's real—our true beauty—takes us in just as we are, and helps us build our lives.

"God sent me here [to the East Coast] because these people don't ask;

they don't seem to care. Moving here was a gift," Margaret says.

My time with Margaret was a gift.

When I met with her that day and we discussed my writing about her, she requested that she remain anonymous. Just for the love of it. So, besides Jesus, Sarah Silverman, and me, all the names in this chapter have been changed to protect their anonymity. Otherwise known as *leggo my ego.*

Little Bunny Cotton Trail

After nearly a year-long break from mountain biking due to a couple of tears in my shoulder and an ornery bout of "frozen shoulder," I recently decided it was time to get back in the saddle. Recovery had been way too slow for my liking, and my shoulder wasn't yet 100 percent, but I was tired of babying it on paved paths. I figured if I kept waiting for my shoulder to fully defrost, I might be waiting forever. This decision was prompted by an experience years ago. I had been recovering from an ankle injury plus surgery, and it wasn't until I started gently pushing myself out of my comfort zone that my ankle got markedly stronger. Post-surgery, I imagined I'd never risk skiing again, for example, but I finally tested *that* out a couple of seasons ago on the famous Utah slopes. I hadn't skied in years but, baby, I screamed down that ~~black diamond~~ bunny hill, good as ever!

Ready to test the ankle theory on my shoulder, I've been back steady on the mountain-biking trail a few weeks now, and so far so good—I'm definitely getting stronger. The ol' shoulder seems to be shouldering things quite well.

Early one morning not long ago, before I headed to the trail, I was warming up on the bedroom floor, doing crunches, stretching, listening to a Bible podcast about the love of Jesus. (I'd been a little better at exercising my heart lately too.) No matter who you are, everyone's life is a mixed bag, filled with good and not so good. The past few years, and especially the past year, have held some full-spectrum events that I would never have imagined could happen—some great, some terrible. My heart has been injured. Torn in more than one place. I will admit, there have been moments I've despaired, felt abandoned, couldn't seem to find the "Jesus love." Had He stopped loving me? Or was it all my fault; did I stray off the path?

Just as my shoulder has been recovering, my heart feels like it might be recovering. In fits and starts perhaps, but recovering, in part because I'd realized I was getting stuck in my pain; frozen, with no range of motion. So I decided to test out my ankle and shoulder theories on my heart. Stop waiting for the pain to go away completely and push myself gently through it. The way I did this was to *not deny the pain* but to stop feeling guilty for it and, at the same time, honestly check myself for moments of counterproductive, indulgent self-pity. To s t r e t c h. To re-direct. To actively invest in deeper, internal work. One simple way was to listen to podcasts such as the one I was hearing this morning about Jesus's love. On the floor, stretching and crunching before, the words were penetrating.

With my Giant bike plastered to the back of my teeny MINI Cooper, I headed out of my neighborhood, down the hill, and stopped behind a car at a red light. To my left, I noticed a man approaching the intersection on the sidewalk. He had on a solid blue T-shirt with white lettering and a *gigantic* smile plastered on his beaming face. Even from that distance, I could see that the proportion of his pearly whites to his head was striking. I don't know if he pushed the "walk" button or not, but his grin was pure joy—as if he just couldn't contain it; as if he had a secret or a treasure; as if he had the best news in the entire world that he yearned to exclaim. Then I noticed the bold white letters on his shirt, exclaiming, "JESUS LOVES YOU."

In the rear-view window of the car ahead of me, I could see the driver's eyes, and he had noticed the man's radiating presence too. I saw them wave to each other. The pedestrian's smile never broke.

As the light turned green and the car entered the intersection, I moved forward. Making eye contact with the man who was still smiling that crazy, joyful smile, I gave him my smile, a nod, and a thumbs up. He returned my gestures. At the very moment that all of this was unfolding, a melodic, almost haunting tune came from my radio. Miraculously synchronized, the music in my car became a soundtrack to the scene I was in with this stranger as the voice in the song repeated, "I should have known, I should have known . . ."

Translated: *Duh, why do you forget?*

I don't claim the writer of those lyrics was speaking of Jesus's love. But I've lived long enough to know that God can use anything He wants to get our attention and declare words of truth. What was coming through my Sirius XM "heavenly" radio were His words, passing through my own heart, speaking aloud as reminders to myself that "I should have known, I should have known." I should have known that Jesus loves me, that He's never left me, that He's loved me all along, even when I stray from the path. I turned the corner at the intersection and began wiping the tears from beneath my sunglasses, tears that flowed the entire two miles to the trailhead.

The trailhead itself quickly descends into a gorge and a series of *whoop-de-doos*, a single track much like a dirt-path roller coaster. I call it Mr. Toad's Wild Ride. Most mountain-biking locals call it "Water Works" because this section is behind and below a water district building. It's challenging, nerve-wracking, and exhilarating, especially for a postmenopausal woman like me who doesn't exactly want to tear anything else on her body but who really likes to have fun.

The trail is a contrast, a true "mixed bag" complete with sudden, vertical hills and drops; twisty-turns; bumps and quick dips; rocks and boulders; dirt and mud; creeks and streams; bright, arid desert; shaded, verdant tropics; and flat sections through sunlit, color-burst meadows.

And you can bet there'll be a proliferation of cottontail bunnies always, no matter which part of the trail or the time of day. However, if you go especially early in the morning, it's crazy-town bunny-wise.

At the parking lot, I removed my bike from the car, put on my helmet and gloves, and headed toward the Wild Ride section. Standing at the precipice, it occurred to me for the first time that I ought to pray before a ride—for protection, that Jesus would be with me. Not only that, that I would feel Him.

I took off, charging down through Mr. Toad's segment, until I got to the bottom and onto the main section of the path. Everywhere along the trail, all the way to O'Neill Campground and back again, there were more cottontails than I'd ever seen before. It reminded me of a sailing trip with my friend Stacie, who was battling brain cancer. On that near-perfect spring day, we got an unforgettable, undeniable dolphin show as they joined us for a ride-along.

It was a taste of *that* on the fourteen miles of mountain-bike trail this day. Instead of a proliferation of dolphins, I was engulfed in bunny rabbits. Cottontails everywhere, bounding and bouncing, scampering back and forth, be-bopping, popping up and down like popcorn. They even showed off by rocketing across the trail an inch in front of my tire over and over again, and then sort of looking back over their bunny shoulder to see if I was impressed.

I was.

As I rode, I noticed their fluffy, pure white tails—all of them with these little puffs of cloud on their bunny butts.

It occurred to me that God didn't have to add the tail, or that He could have added the tail, but did He have to make it such a bright white? Like an exclamation point? It's not like bunnies aren't cute enough. He added that detail for some reason. What was it?

It seems to me that God gets a kick out of the little things, both here on this little bunny cotton trail below the concrete, and above, where strangers stand at traffic lights with other-worldly smiles.

There are so many things we should notice. On any given day, any of these things could remind us that we should have known.

The evidences everywhere . . . those nuances that might go unseen and unfelt if we're not really paying attention, or if our heart is a little frozen and we're just stuck? Maybe these are all part of His tale, ways God is telling His story. *If I don't convince you of My love with a bouncing gray bunny across your path, let Me add a white, fluffy tail as an exclamation point.*

Acknowledgments

Inez—my *big little love* muse.

My husband, John—I've said it before, and I have a hunch I'll keep saying it: you're my biggest cheerleader, who has believed in me always (and all ways); who agreed to take on the coveted moniker "Personal Literary and Publishing Assistant to Ms. Capone"; whom I sometimes call my back-up brain but who's often in reality my main brain. You bring me coffee and so much more.

Libby Kirsch—for your big, prolific brain and big, generous heart and friendship.

Sean Marshall—for being such a fabulous cheerleader, talented writer, inspirer, and friend.

Kris Bearss—my long-suffering yet joyful editor who makes me look way better than I am. (Heads up: I'm going to need you forever, so I hope you're in for the long haul.)

Jill Jones—for proofreading.

Jay Grant—my smart, tenderhearted Scripture consultant and pastor.

Nancy Jernigan—for your insight, efforts, and friendship.

Rob Price and Sarah Spencer at Gatekeeper Press—for printing.

Andrew and Rebecca Brown at Design for Writers—for cover design.

Lisa Parnell at Lisa Parnell Book Services—e-book formatting.

Jeffrey Jansen at Aesthetic Soup—for interior design.

Perla Maarek—for my author photograph.

Kaley Haliburton, Katie Wagner, Stephen Wagner, John Holman, and the entire team at KWSM—for digital marketing.

Terri Green, Jim McNeff, Tony and Lucy DeCaro, Shari Yamamoto, Vicki McCarty, Jamie Johnson, Jamie Randy, Amy Koenig, Kim Towle, Angela Genaro Ruilova, Sherry Tomasula, Nancy Culpepper, Cheryl Potter, Keryn Douglass, Jeni Olsen, Ceitci Demirkova, Christopher and Andrea DeCaro, Mary Creager, and Laraine Tanzer—early book promoters, endorsers, tweeters, and tenacious-lover friends who "volunteered" (*wink, wink*) in various, loving ways on my behalf.

Anyone I may have missed after wracking and wrecking my brain trying to remember everyone—please forgive me, and thank you.

And to all of my examples of tenacious love, ragamuffins, and underdogs as described in my stories (those I interviewed and those I watched from near or afar), who have inspired me and continue to inspire me—I return to you **very big love**.